The Love Poems
of
JOHN DONNE

The Love Poems
of
JOHN DONNE

Edited and introduced by
CHARLES FOWKES

MACMILLAN LONDON

Note to the Reader:
In this edition of John Donne's poetry, spelling has been
modernized and punctuation has been altered to make the
poetry as accessible as possible to the modern reader.

Introduction copyright © 1982 by Charles Fowkes.

This collection first published in the United States 1982 by
St. Martin's Press

First published in the United Kingdom 1983 by
PAPERMAC
a division of Macmillan Publishers Limited
4 Little Essex Street London WC2R 3LF
and Basingstoke

Associated companies in Auckland, Dallas, Delhi, Dublin,
Hong Kong, Johannesburg, Lagos, Manzini, Melbourne,
Nairobi, New York, Singapore, Tokyo, Washington
and Zaria

ISBN 0333 35179 7

Printed in Hong Kong

Design by Dennis J. Grastorf

Contents

ELEGIES

Introduction

MY FIRST COPY of the love poems of John Donne was bought on a winter's evening in London's Charing Cross Road. It may have been bought for me by the girl I was with—I can't remember now. But I do remember that I was in love, and at sixteen it was both exciting and—in a way—comforting to find poems that so perfectly expressed my emotions. A little over a year later "Twickenham Garden" was more relevant to me than *Catcher in the Rye* or any of the other contemporary writing that made up the literary diet of most middle-class adolescents in the mid-sixties: all of which is of no great interest to anyone but me, but it makes two important points. First, that great poetry—although written in the manner of a particular period—is, in an important sense, timeless. Secondly, that the only way I can approach John Donne is personally (which is something the reader needs to know). Scholars have all they need in the impeccable work of Helen Gardner and those who have followed her: Donne has been, and remains, the object of a great deal of critical attention. This collection of the love poetry is for enjoyment, and, as this is the case, academic objectivity is not of the greatest importance. Which is just as well, since I would find such objectivity extremely difficult. It is as if Donne has been lying in wait for me since the purchase of that first book, which I have before me now. He was there when I needed words to express my joy at the marriage of friends, and I remember copying out lines six to ten from "The Anniversary" in a letter. He was waiting for me again when I discovered by accident that he lived in places that I had known well since childhood and that—in a sense—his landscape in Surrey was my own. He was waiting for me again in a New York restaurant when, in conversation with Bob Miller, the idea for this book was first conceived.

* * *

In a letter to the Countess of Bedford, John Donne describes himself as:

> . . . meteor-like, of stuff and form perplexed,
> Whose what and where in disputation is . . .

The simile is interesting from two standpoints: As a simple statement by the poet himself about the nature of his personality, and as a description that is still true today, as we look back at John Donne through four centuries and a plethora of biographical writing ranging from novels to the comprehensive work of Edmund Gosse and R. C. Bald's definitive "life." There is common ground in all the biographies, but John Donne remains elusive. The difficulty does not arise from any shortage of reliable evidence—his life was reasonably well documented—but from the complexity and turbulence of his personality, which often bedevils any straightforward interpretation of the evidence. He was a man full of contradictions, his spirit an unstable amalgam of opposites.

John Donne was born in London in 1572. The family residence, a comfortable merchant's house, was situated on Bread Street, which used to run down to the river from Cheapside. His father was one of the many Welshmen who had come to the capital in the wake of the Tudors; he had made a modest fortune in real estate and as a member of the Worshipful Company of Ironmongers. The Donne family was, therefore, of the same energetic middle-class that produced Shakespeare (whose father was a glover and agricultural merchant) and Spenser (a clothier).

When John Donne was only four his father died. Ben Johnson, writing of the Welsh, asked "whence hath the Crown in all times better servitors, more liberal of their lives and fortunes?" It was certainly true of Donne's father whose will still survives as a record of his kindness and charity. Among several clauses concerned with the distribution of his wealth to the poor and needy, one is particularly revealing:

> To Newgate, Ludgate and the Fleet, the two Compters in
> the Poultry and Woodstreet, and to Bedlam. and to the relief
> of the poor prisoners in the King's Bench, the Marshalry, the
> White Lion and the Compters Southwark, twenty shillings
> apiece.

This concern for the prisoners who languished in London's jails
was more than the charity of a generous man. The Donne family
was Roman Catholic. Elizabeth Donne, John Donne's mother,
was of the persecuted Heywood family and related to the martyr
Sir Thomas More. The misery of incarceration was only too fa-
miliar to all those who had clung to their faith and been "sup-
pressed and afflicted" since the Act of Uniformity.

Less than six months after the death of her first husband, Eliz-
abeth Donne remarried (the haste is best explained by contempo-
rary tax laws). John Donne's stepfather was John Syminges, a
successful physician in his fifties. Like Elizabeth's first husband,
he was probably a Catholic, although this is not certain. What is
certain is that Elizabeth, with most of her family in exile in
Europe, ensured a strict Catholic education for her son. Later,
when he had become an Anglican, Donne wrote in *Pseudo-Martyr:*

> I had a longer work to do than many other men; for I was
> first to blot out certain impressions of the Roman religion,
> and to wrestle both against the examples and against the
> reasons by which some hold was taken, and some anticipa-
> tions early laid, upon my conscience; both by persons who
> by nature had a power and superiority over my will, and
> others who by their learning and good life seemed to me
> justly to claim an interest for the guiding and rectifying of
> mine understanding in these matters.

He makes a point of drawing a distinction between the instruc-
tion he received from a gentle priest (or priests) who taught by
example, and at the hands of a dominating personality in his
family—who could only be his mother.

Elizabeth Donne died only two months before her son, aged about eighty-six. Her character and her relationship with her son—tied up as it was with his religious faith—must be central to any attempt to understand the man. It is significant that his first biographer, Isaac Walton, who knew Donne, his family, and his closest friends, refrains from any full description of the woman. Walton's problem was that he was intent upon seeing everything concerning the late Dean of St. Paul's as sweetness and light—and there was little sweetness and less light in Elizabeth Donne. A comment in one of the sermons may express a painful memory: "And as in the tenderness of our childhood we suffer, yet are whipped if we cry."

The unflinching determination with which Elizabeth Donne remained faithful to her religion and her God despite the banishment and imprisonment of her family does not suggest a soft nature. Her brother, the Jesuit Jasper Heywood, was imprisoned in the Tower under sentence of death (it was later commuted), but even that fearful place could not deter her from visiting him. But the steely singleness of purpose she possessed, while enabling her to resist even the most brutal suppression, was incapable of admitting much gentleness or tolerance within its sphere.

This was the heroic period for the English Catholic martyrs who "kissed the instrument of torture, blessed the hangman and embraced the ladders as they mounted to the gallows" and the son of a Heywood—especially the son of Elizabeth Heywood—had no choice but to take part in this incomprehensible danse macabre.

In October 1584, John, together with his brother Henry, went up to Oxford and was admitted to Hart Hall (which was later to become part of Magdalen College). John was twelve years old, his brother seven. Even for undergraduates of the time, this was a young age to attend university, but Catholic families tended to send their sons to university early. In this way, they could avoid taking the Oath of Supremacy affirming Elizabeth as the head of the Church, which was mandatory at the age of sixteen. For the same reason, Donne left Oxford without a degree, probably in 1588, the year his stepfather died.

Less is known about the next three years than about any period of Donne's life. It is said that he spent a period at Cambridge and that he traveled in Europe; he probably did both. The obscurity of this period suggests that he may have taken advantage of his Catholic connections (at the time, Jasper Heywood was in exile in Naples) and visited Italy and Spain. It is also possible that he saw military service, possibly with Drake and Norreys in the expedition of 1589.

In 1590, the tireless Elizabeth Donne married again. On the sixth of May in the following year her son John entered Thavies Inn (a preparatory school for the law) to be followed shortly afterwards by his brother. The next three years, first at Thavies and then at Lincoln's Inn, saw the first of Donne's mature poetry. As if to register his emergence as an independent adult, he commissioned a portrait, probably by Nicholas Hilliard although only an engraved copy survives. In many ways the engraving gives a more vivid impression of personality than the better-known Newbattle Abbey painting. Donne himself said:

> . . . a hand, or eye
> By Hilliard drawn, is worth a history,
> By a worse painter made.

With his plain clothes and sword, Donne has a rather military appearance in the portrait—perhaps reflecting the manner in which he had spent recent years. The high cheek-bones and strong nose accentuate wide-set eyes that gaze directly at the viewer. The distinct impression created—and presumably intended—is one of challenge and defiance.

It was a period of intense activity for Donne. He himself spoke of his "immoderate desire of human learning"; Walton says that he studied from four in the morning until ten, but then "took great liberty." The young poet was apparently "a great visitor of ladies, a great frequenter of plays." And what a time it was for playgoers, with Shakespeare and Jonson at the beginning of their careers.

Less than a third of the young men at the Inns of Court were ever called to the bar; the main function of the place was to act as an extension to a university education that ended rather early. John Donne studied science, history, politics, languages, and divinity. Walton records that he had become "unresolved what religion to adhere to" and that this was clearly a time of growing conflict in his mind. Donne's Catholic education, if not actually Jesuit, had certainly not been diluted by broadening influences of any kind—the Renaissance humanism that coloured the thinking of Sir Thomas More played no part in his curriculum, which was that of the Counter Reformation. His early training threw any major issue into stark relief—it was either black or white: grays did not appear on the Heywood palette. Consequently no new idea could be assimilated quietly. Each new concept that Donne found in the course of his voracious reading had to be confronted head-on and wrestled with. It did not make for a peaceful existence.

His intellectual and spiritual dilemma was not helped by an intense social frustration that was also, ironically, part of his maternal inheritance. The Heywoods were courtiers, and John Donne's education had been designed to suit him for that role—but as a Catholic his expectations could not be realised. His proximity to the Court, and occasional visits to it, did little to relieve his frustration, but he found some outlet in the satires written at this time:

> Shall I, none's slave, of high-born or raised men
> Fear frowns? and, my mistress Truth, betray thee
> To the huffing braggart, puffed nobility?

The lines seem almost to refer to a slight he had recently received, perhaps at the hands of one of the "raised men" he despises. Earlier in the same satire the criticism is less delicate:

> As prone to all ill, and of good as forgetful,
> As proud, as lustful, and as much in debt,
> As vain, as witless, and as false as they
> Which dwell at Court . . .

No doubt well deserved, the harshness and persistence of the invective nevertheless suggests that special criticism we reserve for what we would secretly wish to have ourselves.

During this same troubled period Donne wrote the majority of the Elegies and a great many of the Songs and Sonnets. It is significant that even the most beautiful of the love poems often have the same energetic, almost aggressive tone. Very few of the love poems are soliloquies; most are addressed to an imagined hearer. There is no escaping the poet—once you have begun to read, he is addressing *you,* and the only way to escape the persistence of the argument is to close the book. In Donne's poetry everything is made to serve the central idea (in a few poems, it has to be said, we could wish for an idea more accessible to the twentieth-century mind), and this includes the meter, which is often uneven, and the language, which is always colloquial. His subject was the many faces of love—his own fickleness, the pain of parting, the agony of secrecy, betrayal by a lover, the exhilaration of sex—but his manner was that of a young lawyer at the Inns of Court: the Songs and Sonnets are advocacy become poetry.

The suppressed energy that characterizes so much of Donne's poetry must have as its source the intellectual, spiritual, and emotional conflict that, throughout his life, he never satisfactorily resolved. The antagonistic forces within the poet's mind would, in less than fifty years, find national expression in the horror of Civil War. If the energy born of conflict found expression in

Donne's poetry, then it also found an outlet in the principal subject of his early work.

Donne's sexuality has been treated strangely by the critics, possibly revealing more about their own proclivities and the fickleness of literary taste than about John Donne. The dominant mother and early replacement of the father, together with an absurdly selective reading of some of the work, has led some latter-day Freudians to hint at homosexuality. None of the so-called evidence (for example, the gender of the speaker in "Break of Day" who is clearly a woman—a device going back to Petrarch and beyond!) is worth serious consideration. Given the tastes of his time, Donne seems to have been markedly heterosexual. He writes a nice epigram on "manliness":

> Thou call'st me effeminate, for I love women's joys;
> I call not thou manly, though thou follow boys.

Another, more serious school, suggests—against what most of us may take to be overwhelming evidence—that "Donne the libertine" had little basis in reality. Obvious truths seem to be little valued by some critics, who weave simplicity into complexity as Rumplestiltskin wove straw into gold because it is the only currency they understand. They take as their text (though it was not intended for this specific purpose) W. H. Auden's statement: "What makes it difficult for a poet not to tell lies is that, in poetry, all facts and all beliefs cease to be true or false and become interesting possibilities." Which is of course true. It is also true that the poetic "I" is often an invention and cannot always be relied upon to indicate personal reminiscence. However, the overwhelming truth lies in the poetry itself—a truth waiting to be released by an unbiased reading of the words. Donne has an uncanny ability to describe a particular moment in time; the poems are full of everyday objects and evocations of particular places: it is not to deny his craftsmanship and creativity to say that he is making an actual event recalled the vehicle (and reason) for a poem. Whether or not the love poems are auto-biographical is a decision each reader must make. If they are not, and Donne was not an intensely sexual man who had known several women before his marriage (and, possibly, after it) then it is hard to explain the lines in "To Christ," arguably his last poem:

> Wilt thou forgive that sin by which I've won
> Others to sin, and made my sin their door?
> Wilt thou forgive that sin which I did shun
> A year or two, but wallowed in a score?

In 1593 a family tragedy exacerbated the conflicts within Donne. His brother Henry was imprisoned for sheltering a priest. It was a terrible year. London was smitten by plague, with over fifteen thousand deaths in the capital alone. In such times persecution is all too often the response, and in late sixteenth-century England the victims of persecution were the Catholics: "There is no room for thieves in the prisons . . . there are so many Catholics." Henry Donne died in Newgate, having contracted either plague or jail fever.

The event finally isolated John Donne from his mother and his family. Quite alone now, and with the help of his brother's share of their inheritance, he set about building his own life. In the years between 1593 and the turn of the century Donne sailed with Raleigh and Essex in the expedition to Cadiz, and, later, to the Azores. If the sensual Newbattle Abbey portrait is any guide, the life of libertinism continued from his new lodgings in the Strand. By this time his circumstances had improved sufficiently for him to hire a servant, and he had himself entered the service of the Lord Keeper of England, Sir Thomas Egerton. This was to be the most creative period of his life: Walton says that all his best work was done before he was twenty-five.

In 1602 John Donne's rising fortunes were cruelly dashed: Egerton dismissed him, and he was, like his brother, thrown into prison—but for quite a different reason. His crime was that he had secretly married Ann More, daughter of Sir George More who was Sir Thomas Egerton's brother-in-law. Ann was seventeen and a minor, and her father's permission had not been sought. It had not been sought because it would not have been given. Loseley, Sir George More's great house to the south of Guildford, had been visited several times by the Virgin Queen herself. A marriage between a daughter of the house and Donne would not have pleased the ambitious man who was already the Member of Parliament for Guildford as well as High Sherriff of Surrey and Sussex. Ann and John Donne had been lovers for over a year before they married. Whether some of the love poems record their secret relationship in York House (Egerton's magnificent residence on the Thames near present-day Hungerford Bridge) is for the reader to decide.

Eventually Sir George More recanted, but evidently not before he had become vicious. In a letter sent to him after his release from prison Donne says that the charges "of having deceived some gentlewoman before, and that of loving a corrupt religion, are vanished and smoked away."

Reunited, their marriage accepted as legal, the couple moved to Pyrford in Surrey to live in the house of Francis Wolley, a friend who had accompanied Donne on the expedition to the Azores and who was Ann's cousin. Living by patronage is not comfortable, but it was to be Donne's way of life until his ordination in 1615. Their first two children were born at Pyrford. They were probably baptized in the little Norman church of St. Nicholas, and Donne would have been familiar with the twelfth-century wall paintings depicting the Flagellation of Christ and the Battle between Good and Evil. (Behind the beautiful church, where the graveyard overlooks the crossing of the River Wey, Cromwell set up his cannon to bombard the Royalist stronghold of Neward Priory in the darkest days of the Civil War.)

In 1605, eighteen months after the accession of James and the year of the Gunpowder Plot, the Donne family moved to Mitcham. Today the town is a southern suburb of London, but in the early part of the seventeenth century it was a small village in the country, a long ride from the capital and, therefore, unfashionable and cheap. Most of the inhabitants of Mitcham lived by farming and by grazing stock on the great common which is today more or less unchanged except that it is bisected by the South Western Railway. It is sad, flat country, drained by the River Wandle. Donne complained of the "barbarousness and insipid dullness of the country. . . . I that live in the country without stupefying, am not in darkness, but in shadow, which is not light, but a pallid, waterish and diluted one."

Each year brought a new baby and a further drain on the physical and financial resources of the family. Donne, who hated his "thin little house" traveled as much as possible, abroad on occasions, constantly endeavoring to find a post that would provide a better life for them. Two extracts from letters sent to friends sum up their life at Mitcham:

> I write from the fireside in my parlour, and in the noise of three gamesome children; and by the side of her, whom because I have transplanted into a wretched fortune, I must labour to disguise that from her by all such honest devices, as by giving her my company, and discourse, and therefore I steal from her, all the time which I give this letter, and it is therefore that I take so short a list and gallop so fast over it . . .

Although a tiny part of his great fortune could have relieved the misery in which they lived—Donne trying to write while damp vapors rose up from the cellar and made his joints ache—Sir George More had made it clear when he grudgingly acknowledged the marriage that Ann could expect no dowry of any kind. In another letter, following a miscarriage and when he was the only healthy person in the house, Donne writes:

> My wife is fallen into such a discomposure as would afflict her too extremely, but that the sickness of all her other chil-

dren stupefies her; of one of which, in good faith I have not much hope; and these meet with fortune so ill-provided for physic and such relief, that if God should ease us with burials, I know not how to perform even that . . .

In 1612 the Donne family left Mitcham for a house on the estate of Sir Robert Drury in Drury Lane. Largely in gratitude for three poems that Donne had written about the death of his only daughter, Sir Robert made the tenancy rent-free. This new patronage quite changed the family's way of living. Comfortable surroundings and the stimulus of travel and intelligent society lifted Donne from the depression he had known at Mitcham. The recharging of his emotional and physical batteries was timely. Within three years he had taken the most important step in his life. Under the influence of the polemicist Thomas Morton, and with King James himself flattering and conniving, the scales were tipped. On the twenty-third of January, 1615, John Donne, born a Catholic, was ordained deacon and priest in the Church of England. The ceremony took place in St. Paul's Cathedral, the great church of which he was to become dean in 1621 and in which he was buried with great ceremony in April 1631.

In the intervening years, out of the torment and conflict that never left him, he wrote some of the greatest Christian sermons in the language and some of the most powerful religious poetry. "Holy Sonnet XIV" is unlike any other religious poetry ever written, a challenge to God, from one who believes he has the right to challenge:

> Batter my heart, three-personed God; for, you
> As yet but knock, breathe, shine and seek to mend;
> That I may rise, and stand, o'erthrow me, and bend
> Your force, to break, blow, burn and make me new.
> I, like an usurped town, to another due,
> Labour to admit you, but Oh, to no end,
> Reason your viceroy in me, me should defend,
> But is captived, and proves weak or untrue.

Yet dearly I love you, and would be loved fain,
But am betrothed unto your enemy:
Divorce me, untie, or break that knot again,
Take me to you, imprison me, for I
Except you enthral me, never shall be free,
Nor ever chaste, except you ravish me!

As magnificent as this poem—and much of the other religious writing—is, some of the religious poetry Donne wrote toward the end of his life is clearly the product of an intellect whose power has turned upon itself: the outpourings of a great poet wallowing in misery and guilt.

Perhaps it need not have been so. But in the summer of 1617, after giving birth to a still-born child, Ann died. John Donne wrote a sonnet upon his wife's death. Although normally included among the religious poetry, it is also the last of the love poems:

Since she whom I loved hath payed her last debt
To nature, and to hers, and my good is dead,
And her soul early into heaven ravished,
Wholly on heavenly things my mind is set.
Here the admiring her my mind did whet
To seek thee God; so streams do show their head,
But though I have found thee, and thou my thirst hath fed,
A holy thirsty dropsy melts me yet.

But why should I beg more love, when as thou
Dost woo my soul for hers; offering all thine:
And dost not only fear lest I allow
My love to saints and angels, things divine,
But in thy tender jealousy dost doubt
Lest the world, flesh, yea Devil put thee out.

CHARLES FOWKES

London, 1982

The Love Poems
of

JOHN DONNE

The Good-morrow

I wonder by my troth, what thou and I
Did, till we loved? were we not weaned till then,
But sucked on country pleasures, childishly?
Or snorted we in the seven sleepers' den?
'Twas so; but this, all pleasures fancies be.
If ever any beauty I did see,
Which I desired,and got, 'twas but a dream of thee.

And now good-morrow to our waking souls,
Which watch not one another out of fear,
For love all love of other sights controls,
And makes one little room, an everywhere.
Let sea-discoverers to new worlds have gone,
Let maps to other, worlds on worlds have shown,
Let us possess one world, each hath one, and is one.

My face in thine eye, thine in mine appears,
And true plain hearts do in the faces rest;
Where can we find two better hemispheres
Without sharp North, without declining West?
What ever dies, was not mixed equally;
If our two loves be one, or thou and I
Love so alike that none do slacken, none can die.

Song

Go, and catch a falling star,
   Get with child a mandrake root,
Tell me, where all past years are,
   Or who cleft the Devil's foot,
Teach me to hear Mermaids singing,
   Or to keep off envy's stinging,
         And find
         What wind
Serves to advance an honest mind.

If thou beest born to strange sights,
   Things invisible to see,
Ride ten thousand days and nights,
   Till age snow white hairs on thee,
Thou, when thou return'st, wilt tell me
All strange wonders that befell thee,
         And swear
         No where
Lives a woman true, and fair.

If thou find'st one, let me know,
   Such a Pilgrimage were sweet;
Yet do not, I would not go,
   Though at next door we might meet,
Though she were true, when you met her,
And last, till you write your letter,
         Yet she
         Will be
False, ere I come, to two, or three.

Woman's Constancy

Now thou hast loved me one whole day,
Tomorrow when thou leav'st, what wilt thou say?
Wilt thou then antedate some new made vow?
        Or say that now
We are not just those persons, which we were?
Or, that oaths made in reverential fear
Of Love, and his wrath, any may forswear?
Or, as true deaths true marriages untie,
So lovers' contracts, images of those,
Bind but till sleep, death's image, them unloose?
        Or, your own end to justify,
For having purposed change, and falsehood, you
Can have no way but falsehood to be true?
Vain lunatic, against these 'scapes I could
        Dispute, and conquer, if I would,
        Which I abstain to do,
For by tomorrow, I may think so too.

The Undertaking

I have done one braver thing
  Than all the *Worthies* did,
And yet a braver thence doth spring,
  Which is, to keep that hid.

It were but madness now to impart
  The skill of specular stone,
When he which can have learned the art
  To cut it, can find none.

So, if I now should utter this,
  Others (because no more
Such stuff to work upon, there is,)
  Would love but as before.

But he who loveliness within
  Hath found, all outward loathes,
For he who colour loves, and skin,
  Loves but their oldest clothes.

If, as I have, you also do
  Virtue attired in woman see,
And dare love that, and say so too,
  And forget the He and She;

And if this love, though placed so,
  From profane men you hide,
Which will no faith on this bestow,
  Or, if they do, deride:

Then you have done a braver thing
  Than all the *Worthies* did;
And a braver thence will spring,
  Which is, to keep that hid.

The Sun Rising

Busy old fool, unruly Sun,
  Why dost thou thus,
Through windows, and through curtains call on us?
Must to thy motions lovers' seasons run?
  Saucy, pedantic wretch, go chide
  Late school-boys, and sour prentices,
 Go tell Court-huntsmen, that the King will ride,
 Call country ants to harvest offices;
Love, all alike, no season knows, nor clime,
Nor hours, days, months, which are the rags of time.

  Thy beams so reverend, and strong
  Why shouldst thou think?
I could eclipse and cloud them with a wink,
But that I would not lose her sight so long:
  If her eyes have not blinded thine,
  Look, and tomorrow late, tell me,
 Whether both the Indias of spice and mine
 Be where thou left'st them, or lie here with me.
Ask for those Kings whom thou saw'st yesterday,
And thou shalt hear, All here in one bed lay.

  She's all states, and all princes, I,
  Nothing else is.
Princes do but play us; compared to this,
All honour's mimic; all wealth alchemy.
  Thou sun art half as happy as we,
  In that the world's contracted thus;
 Thine age asks ease, and since thy duties be
 To warm the world, that's done in warming us.
Shine here to us, and thou art everywhere;
This bed thy centre is, these walls, thy sphere.

The Indifferent

I can love both fair and brown,
Her whom abundance melts, and her whom want betrays,
Her who loves loneness best, and her who masks and plays,
Her whom the country formed, and whom the town,
Her who believes, and her who tries,
Her who still weeps with spongy eyes,
And her who is dry cork, and never cries;
I can love her, and her, and you and you,
I can love any, so she be not true.

Will no other vice content you?
Will it not serve your turn to do as did your mothers?
Or have you all old vices spent, and now would find out
    others?
Or doth a fear, that men are true, torment you?
Oh we are not, be not you so;
Let me, and do you, twenty know.
Rob me, but bind me not, and let me go.
Must I, who came to travail thorough you,
Grow your fixed subject, because you are true?

Venus heard me sigh this song,
And by Love's sweetest part, Variety, she swore
She heard not this till now; and that it should be so no more.
She went, examined, and returned ere long,
And said, alas, some two or three
Poor heretics in love there be,
Which think to establish dangerous constancy.
But I have told them: since you will be true,
You shall be true to them, who're false to you.

Love's Usury

*F*or every hour that thou wilt spare me now,
      I will allow,
Usurious God of Love, twenty to thee,
When with my brown, my gray hairs equal be;
Till then, Love, let my body reign, and let
Me travel sojourn, snatch, plot, have, forget,
Resume my last year's relict: think that yet
      We'd never met.

Let me think any rival's letter mine,
      And at next nine
Keep midnight's promise; mistake by the way
The maid, and tell the Lady of that delay;
Only let me love none, no, not the sport;
From country grass, to comfitures of Court,
Or city's *quelque-choses,* let report
      My mind transport.

This bargain's good; if when I'm old, I be
      Inflamed by thee,
If thine own honour, or my shame, or pain,
Thou covet most, at that age thou shalt gain.
Do thy will then, then subject and degree,
And fruit of love, Love, I submit to thee;
Spare me till then, I'll bear it, though she be
      One that loves me.

The Canonization

For God's sake hold your tongue, and let me love;
  Or chide my palsy, or my gout,
My five gray hairs, or ruined fortune flout;
    With wealth your state, your mind with arts improve,
      Take you a course, get you a place,
      Observe his Honour, or his Grace,
Or the King's real, or his stamped face.
    Contemplate; what you will, approve,
    So you will let me love.

Alas, alas, who's injured by my love?
  What merchant's ship have my sighs drowned
Who says my tears have overflowed his ground?
    When did my colds a forward spring remove?
      When did the heats which my veins fill
      Add one more to the plaguy bill?
Soldiers find wars, and lawyers find out still
  Litigious men, which quarrels move,
  Though she and I do love.

Call us what you will, we are made such by love;
  Call her one, me another fly,
We're tapers too, and at our own cost die,
    And we in us find the Eagle and the Dove.
      The Phoenix riddle hath more wit
      By us; we two being one, are it.
So to one neutral thing both sexes fit,
  We die and rise the same, and prove
  Mysterious by this love.

We can die by it, if not live by love,
    And if unfit for tombs and hearse
Our legend be, it will be fit for verse;
    And if no piece of chronicle we prove,
        We'll build in sonnets pretty rooms;
        As well a well-wrought urn becomes
The greatest ashes, as half-acre tombs,
    And by these hymns, all shall approve
    Us canonized for love:

And thus invoke us; You whom reverend love
    Made one another's hermitage;
You, to whom love was peace, that now is rage;
    Who did the whole world's soul contract, and drove
        Into the glasses of your eyes
        (So made such mirrors, and such spies,
    That they did all to you epitomize,)
        Countries, towns, courts: beg from above
        A pattern of your love!

The Triple Fool

I am two fools, I know,
For loving, and for saying so
 In whining poetry;
But where's that wise man, that would not be I,
 If she would not deny?
Then as th' earth's inward narrow crooked lanes
Do purge sea-water's fretful salt away,
 I thought, if I could draw my pains
Through rhyme's vexation, I should them allay.
Grief brought to numbers cannot be so fierce,
For he tames it, that fetters it in verse.

 But when I have done so,
Some man, his art and voice to show,
 Doth set and sing my pain,
And, by delighting many, frees again
 Grief, which verse did restrain.
To Love and Grief tribute of Verse belongs,
But not of such as pleases when 'tis read;
 Both are increased by such songs:
For both their triumphs so are published,
And I, which was two fools, do so grow three;
Who are a little wise, the best fools be.

Lovers' Infiniteness

If yet I have not all thy love,
Dear, I shall never have it all,
I cannot breathe one other sigh, to move,
Nor can entreat one other tear to fall,
And all my treasure, which should purchase thee,
Sighs, tears, and oaths, and letters I have spent.
Yet no more can be due to me,
Than at the bargain made was meant.
If then thy gift of love were partial,
That some to me, some should to others fall,
    Dear, I shall never have thee all.

Or if then thou gavest me all,
All was but all, which thou hadst then;
But if in thy heart, since, there be or shall
New love created be, by other men,
Which have their stocks entire, and can in tears,
In sighs, in oaths, and letters outbid me,
This new love may beget new fears,
For, this love was not vowed by thee.
And yet it was, thy gift being general;
The ground, thy heart, is mine; whatever shall
    Grow there, dear, I should have it all.

Yet I would not have all yet,
He that hath all can have no more,
And since my love doth every day admit
New growth, thou shouldst have new rewards in store;
Thou canst not every day give me thy heart,
If thou canst give it, then thou never gavest it:
Love's riddles are, that though thy heart depart,
It stays at home, and thou with losing savest it:
But we will have a way more liberal,
Than changing hearts, to join them, so we shall
    Be one, and one another's all.

Song

Sweetest love, I do not go,
    For weariness of thee,
Nor in hope the world can show
    A fitter love for me;
        But since that I
Must die at last, 'tis best,
To use my self in jest
    Thus by feigned deaths to die.

Yesternight the Sun went hence;
    And yet is here today;
He hath no desire nor sense;
    Nor half so short a way:
        Then fear not me,
But believe that I shall make
Speedier journeys, since I take
    More wings and spurs than he.

O how feeble is man's power,
    That if good fortune fall,
Cannot add another hour,
    Nor a lost hour recall!
        But come bad chance,
And we join to it our strength
And we teach it art and length,
    Itself o'er us to advance.

When thou sigh'st, thou sigh'st not wind,
    But sigh'st my soul away,
When thou weepest, unkindly kind,
    My life's blood doth decay.
        It cannot be
That thou lovest me, as thou sayest,
If in thine my life thou waste,
    Thou art the best of me.

Let not thy divining heart
  Forethink me any ill,
Destiny may take thy part,
  And may thy fears fulfil;
    But think that we
Are but turned aside to sleep;
They who one another keep
    Alive, ne'er parted be.

The Legacy

When I died last, and, dear, I die
  As often as from thee I go,
  Though it be but an hour ago,
And lovers' hours be full eternity,
I can remember yet, that I
  Something did say, and something did bestow;
Though I be dead, which sent me, I should be
Mine own executor and legacy.

I heard me say: 'Tell her anon,
  That my self, (that is you, not I,)
  Did kill me,' and when I felt me die,
I bid me send my heart, when I was gone;
But I alas could there find none,
  When I had ripped me, and searched where hearts did lie;
It killed me again, that I who still was true,
In life, in my last will should cozen you.

Yet I found something like a heart,
  But colours it, and corners had,
  It was not good, it was not bad,
It was entire to none, and few had part.
As good as could be made by art
  It seemed; and therefore for our losses sad,
I meant to send this heart instead of mine,
But oh, no man could hold it, for 'twas thine.

A Fever

Oh do not die, for I shall hate
   All women so, when thou art gone,
That thee I shall not celebrate,
   When I remember, thou wast one.

But yet thou canst not die, I know,
   To leave this world behind, is death,
But when thou from this world wilt go,
   The whole world vapours with thy breath.

Or if, when thou, the world's soul, goest,
   It stay, 'tis but thy carcase then,
The fairest woman, but thy ghost,
   But corrupt worms, the worthiest men.

O wrangling schools, that search what fire
   Shall burn this world, had none the wit
Unto this knowledge to aspire,
   That this her fever might be it?

And yet she cannot waste by this,
   Nor long bear this torturing wrong,
For such corruption needful is
   To fuel such a fever long.

These burning fits but meteors be,
   Whose matter in thee is soon spent.
Thy beauty, and all parts, which are thee,
   Are unchangeable firmament.

Yet 'twas of my mind, seizing thee,
   Though it in thee cannot persever.
For I had rather owner be
   Of thee one hour, than all else ever.

Air and Angels

*T*wice or thrice had I loved thee,
Before I knew thy face or name;
So in a voice, so in a shapeless flame,
Angels affect us oft, and worshipped be;
   Still when, to where thou wert, I came,
Some lovely glorious nothing I did see.
   But since my soul, whose child love is,
Takes limbs of flesh, and else could nothing do,
   More subtle than the parent is,
Love must not be, but take a body too,
   And therefore what thou wert, and who,
     I bid Love ask, and now
That it assume thy body, I allow,
And fix itself in thy lip, eye, and brow.

Whilst thus to ballast love, I thought,
And so more steadily to have gone,
With wares which would sink admiration,
I saw, I had love's pinnace overfraught;
   Every thy hair for love to work upon
Is much too much, some fitter must be sought;
   For, nor in nothing, nor in things
Extreme, and scattering bright, can love inhere;
   Then as an Angel, face and wings
Of air, not pure as it, yet pure doth wear,
   So thy love may be my love's sphere;
     Just such disparity
As is 'twixt Air and Angels' purity,
'Twixt women's love, and men's will ever be.

Break of Day

'Tis true, 'tis day; what though it be?
O wilt thou therefore rise from me?
Why should we rise, because 'tis light?
Did we lie down, because 'twas night?
Love which in spite of darkness brought us hither,
Should in despite of light keep us together.

Light hath no tongue, but is all eye;
If it could speak as well as spy,
This were the worst, that it could say,
That being well, I fain would stay,
And that I loved my heart and honour so,
That I would not from him, that had them, go.

Must business thee from hence remove?
Oh, that's the worst disease of love,
The poor, the foul, the false, love can
Admit, but not the busied man.
He which hath business, and makes love, doth do
Such wrong, as when a married man doth woo.

The Anniversary

All kings, and all their favourites,
    All glory of honours, beauties, wits,
The Sun itself, which makes times, as they pass,
Is elder by a year, now, than it was
When thou and I first one another saw:
All other things to their destruction draw,
    Only our love hath no decay;
This, no tomorrow hath, nor yesterday,
Running it never runs from us away,
But truly keeps his first, last, everlasting day.

    Two graves must hide thine and my corse,
    If one might, death were no divorce.
Alas, as well as other princes, we,
(Who prince enough in one another be,)
Must leave at last in death, these eyes, and ears,
Oft fed with true oaths, and with sweet salt tears;
    But souls where nothing dwells but love
(All other thoughts being inmates) then shall prove
This, or a love increased there above,
When bodies to their graves, souls from their graves remove.

    And then we shall be throughly blest,
    But we no more, than all the rest;
Here upon earth, we're kings, and none but we
Can be such kings, nor of such subjects be.
Who is so safe as we? where none can do
Treason to us, except one of us two.
    True and false fears let us refrain,
Let us love nobly, and live, and add again
Years and years unto years, till we attain
To write threescore: this is the second of our reign.

A Valediction: Of My Name, in the Window

I

*M*y name engraved herein
Doth contribute my firmness to this glass,
   Which, ever since that charm, hath been
   As hard as that which graved it was;
Thine eye will give it price enough, to mock
      The diamonds of either rock.

II

'Tis much that glass should be
As all-confessing, and through-shine as I,
   'Tis more, that it shows thee to thee,
   And clear reflects thee to thine eye.
But all such rules, love's magic can undo,
      Here you see me, and I am you.

III

As no one point, nor dash,
Which are but accessories to this name,
   The showers and tempests can outwash,
   So shall all times find me the same;
You this entireness better may fulfil,
      Who have the pattern with you still.

IV

Or if too hard and deep
This learning be, for a scratched name to teach,
   It, as a given death's head keep,
   Lovers' mortality to preach,
Or think this ragged bony name to be
      My ruinous anatomy.

V

Then, as all my souls be
Emparadised in you, (in whom alone
I understand, and grow and see,)
The rafters of my body, bone
Being still with you, the muscle, sinew, and vein,
Which tile this house, will come again.

VI

Till my return, repair
And recompact my scattered body so.
As all the virtuous powers which are
Fixed in the stars, are said to flow
Into such characters, as graved be
When these stars have supremacy:

VII

So since this name was cut
When love and grief their exaltation had,
No door against this name's influence shut;
As much more loving, as more sad,
'Twill make thee; and thou shouldst, till I return,
Since I die daily, daily mourn.

VIII

When thy inconsiderate hand
Flings ope this casement, with my trembling name,
To look on one, whose wit or land,
New battery to thy heart may frame,
Then think this name alive, and that thou thus
In it offend'st my Genius.

IX

And when thy melted maid,
Corrupted by thy lover's gold, and page,
His letter at thy pillow hath laid,
Disputed it, and tamed thy rage,
And thou begin'st to thaw towards him, for this,
May my name step in, and hide his.

X

And if this treason go
To an overt act, and that thou write again;
  In superscribing, this name flow
  Into thy fancy, from the pane.
So, in forgetting thou rememberest right,
      And unaware to me shalt write.

XI

But glass and lines must be
No means our firm substantial love to keep;
  Near death inflicts this lethargy.
  And this I murmur in my sleep;
Impute this idle talk, to that I go,
      For dying men talk often so.

Twickenham Garden

*B*lasted with sighs, and surrounded with tears,
    Hither I come to seek the spring,
    And at mine eyes, and at mine ears,
Receive such balms, as else cure everything;
    But O, self-traitor, I do bring
The spider love, which transubstantiates all,
    And can convert manna to gall,
And that this place may thoroughly be thought
    True Paradise, I have the serpent brought.

'Twere wholesomer for me, that winter did
    Benight the glory of this place,
    And that a grave frost did forbid
These trees to laugh, and mock me to my face;
    But that I may not this disgrace
Endure, nor yet leave loving, Love, let me
    Some senseless piece of this place be;
Make me a mandrake, so I may groan here,
    Or a stone fountain weeping out my year.

Hither with crystal vials, lovers come,
    And take my tears, which are love's wine,
And try your mistress' tears at home,
For all are false, that taste not just like mine;
    Alas, hearts do not in eyes shine,
Nor can you more judge woman's thoughts by tears,
    Than by her shadow, what she wears.
O perverse sex, where none is true but she,
    Who's therefore true, because her truth kills me.

A Valediction: Of the Book

I'll tell thee now (dear Love) what thou shalt do
   To anger destiny, as she doth us,
   How I shall stay, though she esloign me thus,
And how posterity shall know it too;
     How thine may out-endure
     Sibyl's glory, and obscure
     Her who from *Pindar* could allure,
   And her, through whose help *Lucan* is not lame,
And her, whose book (they say) *Homer* did find, and name.

Study our manuscripts, those myriads
   Of letters, which have past 'twixt thee and me,
   Thence write our annals, and in them will be
To all whom love's subliming fire invades,
     Rule and example found;
     There, the faith of any ground
     No schismatic will dare to wound,
   That sees, how Love this grace to us affords,
To make, to keep, to use, to be these his records.

This book, as long-lived as the elements,
   Or as the world's form, this all-graved tome
   In cypher writ, or new made idiom,
We for Love's clergy only are instruments:
     When this book is made thus,
     Should again the ravenous
     Vandals and Goths inundate us,
   Learning were safe; in this our universe
Schools might learn sciences, spheres music, angels verse.

Here Love's divines (since all divinity
   Is love or wonder) may find all they seek,
   Whether abstract spiritual love they like,
Their souls exhaled with what they do not see,
      Or, loth so to amuse
      Faith's infirmity, they choose
      Something which they may see and use;
   For, though mind be the heaven, where love doth sit,
Beauty a convenient type may be to figure it.

Here more than in their books may lawyers find,
   Both by what titles mistresses are ours,
   And how prerogative these states devours,
Transferred from Love himself, to womankind,
      Who though from heart, and eyes,
      They exact great subsidies,
      Forsake him who on them relies,
   And for the cause, honour, or conscience give,
Chimeras, vain as they, or their prerogative.

Here statesmen, (or of them, they which can read,)
   May of their occupation find the grounds:
   Love and their art alike it deadly wounds,
If to consider what 'tis, one proceed,
      In both they do excel
      Who the present govern well,
      Whose weakness none doth, or dares tell;
   In this thy book, such will their nothing see,
As in the Bible some can find out alchemy.

Thus vent thy thoughts; abroad I'll study thee,
   As he removes far off, that great heights takes;
   How great love is, presence best trial makes,
But absence tries how long this love will be;
      To take a latitude
      Sun, or stars, are fitliest viewed
      At their brightest, but to conclude
   Of longitudes, what other way have we,
But to mark when, and where the dark eclipses be?

Community

Good we must love, and must hate ill,
For ill is ill, and good good still,
    But there are things indifferent,
Which we may neither hate, nor love,
But one, and then another prove,
    As we shall find our fancy bent.

If then at first wise Nature had
Made women either good or bad,
    Then some we might hate, and some choose,
But since she did them so create,
That we may neither love, nor hate,
    Only this rests, All, all may use.

If they were good it would be seen,
Good is as visible as green,
    And to all eyes itself betrays:
If they were bad, they could not last,
Bad doth itself and others waste;
    So, they deserve nor blame, nor praise.

But they are ours as fruits are ours,
He that but tastes, he that devours,
    And he that leaves all, doth as well:
Changed loves are but changed sorts of meat,
And when he hath the kernel eat,
    Who doth not fling away the shell?

Love's Growth

I scarce believe my love to be so pure
    As I had thought it was,
    Because it doth endure
Vicissitude, and season, as the grass;
Methinks I lied all winter; when I swore,
My love was infinite, if spring make it more.
But if this medicine, love, which cures all sorrow
With more, not only be no quintessence,
But mixed of all stuffs, paining soul, or sense,
And of the Sun his working vigour borrow,
Love's not so pure, and abstract, as they use
To say, which have no mistress but their Muse,
But as all else, being elemented too,
Love sometimes would contemplate, sometimes do.

And yet no greater, but more eminent,
    Love by the Spring is grown;
    As, in the firmament,
Stars by the Sun are not enlarged, but shown,
Gentle love deeds, as blossoms on a bough,
From love's awakened root do bud out now.
If, as in water stirred more circles be
Produced by one, love such additions take,
Those like so many spheres, but one heaven make,
For, they are all concentric unto thee.
And though each spring do add to love new heat,
As princes do in times of action get
New taxes, and remit them not in peace,
No winter shall abate the Spring's increase.

Love's Exchange

Love, any devil else but you,
Would for a given soul give something too.
At Court your fellows every day,
Give th' art of rhyming, huntsmanship, or play,
For them which were their own before;
Only I have nothing which gave more,
But am, alas, by being lowly, lower.

I ask no dispensation now
To falsify a tear, or sigh, or vow,
I do not sue from thee to draw
A *non obstante* on nature's law,
These are preogatives, they inhere
In thee and thine; none should forswear
Except that he Love's minion were.

Give me thy weakness, make me blind,
Both ways, as thou and thine, in eyes and mind;
Love, let me never know that this
Is love, or, that love childish is.
Let me not know that others know
That she knows my pains, lest that so
A tender shame make me mine own new woe.

If thou give nothing, yet thou'rt just,
Because I would not thy first motions trust;
Small towns which stand stiff, till great shot
Enforce them, by war's law condition not.
Such in love's warfare is my case,
I may not article for grace,
Having put Love at last to show this face.

This face, by which he could command
And change the idolatry of any land,
This face, which whereso'er it comes,
Can call vowed men from cloisters, dead from tombs,
And melt both Poles at once, and store
Deserts with cities, and make more
Mines in the earth, than quarries were before.

For this, Love is enraged with me,
Yet kills not. If I must example be
To future rebels; if the unborn
Must learn, by my being cut up, and torn:
Kill, and dissect me, Love; for this
Torture against thine own end is,
Racked carcases make ill anatomies.

Confined Love

Some man unworthy to be possessor
Of old or new love, himself being false or weak,
  Thought his pain and shame would be lesser,
If on womankind he might his anger wreak,
        And thence a law did grow,
        One might but one man know;
        But are other creatures so?

  Are Sun, Moon, or Stars by law forbidden,
To smile where they list, or lend away their light?
  Are birds divorced, or are they chidden
If they leave their mate, or lie abroad a-night?
        Beasts do no jointures lose
        Though they new lovers choose,
        But we are made worse than those.

  Who e'er rigged fair ship to lie in harbours
And not to seek new lands, or not to deal withal?
  Or built fair houses, set trees, and arbours,
Only to lock up, or else to let them fall?
        Good is not good, unless
        A thousand it possess,
        But doth waste with greediness.

The Dream

Dear love, for nothing less than thee
Would I have broke this happy dream,
      It was a theme
For reason, much too strong for phantasy,
Therefore thou waked'st me wisely; yet
My dream thou brokest not, but continued'st it;
Thou art so truth, that thoughts of thee suffice,
To make dreams truths, and fables histories;
Enter these arms, for since thou thought'st it best,
Not to dream all my dream, let's act the rest.

As lightning, or a taper's light,
Thine eyes, and not thy noise waked me;
      Yet I thought thee
(For thou lovest truth) an angel, at first sight,
But when I saw thou sawest my heart,
And knew'st my thoughts, beyond an angel's art,
When thou knew'st what I dreamt, when thou knew'st
    when
Excess of joy would wake me, and cam'st then,
I must confess, it could not choose but be
Profane, to think thee anything but thee.

Coming and staying showed thee, thee,
But rising makes me doubt, that now,
      Thou art not thou.
That love is weak, where fear's as strong as he;
'Tis not all spirit, pure, and brave,
If mixture it of *Fear, Shame, Honour,* have.
Perchance as torches which must ready be,
Men light and put out, so thou deal'st with me,
Thou cam'st to kindle, goest to come; then I
Will dream that hope again, but else would die.

A Valediction: Of Weeping

Let me pour forth
My tears before thy face, whilst I stay here,
For thy face coins them, and thy stamp they bear,
And by this mintage they are something worth,
         For thus they be
         Pregnant of thee;
Fruits of much grief they are, emblems of more;
When a tear falls, that thou falls which it bore,
So thou and I are nothing then, when on a divers shore

         On a round ball
A workman that hath copies by, can lay
An Europe, Afric, and an Asia,
And quickly make that, which was nothing, *All*,
         So doth each tear,
         Which thee doth wear.
A globe, yea world by that impression grow,
Till thy tears mixt with mine do overflow
This world, by waters sent from thee, my heaven dissolved so.

         O more than Moon,
Draw not up seas to drown me in thy sphere,
Weep me not dead, in thine arms, but forbear
To teach the sea, what it may do too soon;
         Let not the wind
         Example find,
To do me more harm, than it purposeth;
Since thou and I sigh one another's breath,
Whoe'er sighs most, is cruellest, and hastes the other's death

Love's Alchemy

Some that have deeper digged love's mine than I,
Say, where his centric happiness doth lie.
      I have loved, and got, and told,
But should I love, get, tell, till I were old,
I should not find that hidden mystery;
      Oh, 'tis imposture all:
And as no chemic yet th' elixir got,
      But glorifies his pregnant pot,
      If by the way to him befall
Some odoriferous thing, or medicinal,
  So, lovers dream a rich and long delight,
  But get a winter-seeming summer's night.

Our case, our thrift, our honour, and our day,
Shall we, for this vain bubble's shadow pay?
      Ends love in this, that my man,
Can be as happy as I can; if he can
Endure the short scorn of a bridegroom's play?
      That loving wretch that swears,
'Tis not the bodies marry, but the minds,
      Which he in her angelic finds,
      Would swear as justly, that he hears,
In that day's rude hoarse minstrelsy, the spheres.
Hope not for mind in women; at their best
  Sweetness and wit, they are but *Mummy,* possessed.

The Flea

Mark but this flea, and mark in this,
How little that which thou deny'st me is;
It sucked me first, and now sucks thee,
And in this flea, our two bloods mingled be;
Thou knowest that this cannot be said
A sin, nor shame, nor loss of maidenhead,
   Yet this enjoys before it woo,
    And pampered swells with one blood made of two,
    And this, alas, is more than we would do.

Oh stay, three lives in one flea spare,
Where we almost, yea more than married are.
This flea is you and I, and this
Our marriage bed, and marriage temple is;
Though parents grudge, and you, we're met,
And cloistered in these living walls of jet.
   Though use make you apt to kill me,
    Let not to that, self murder added be,
    And sacrilege, three sins in killing three.

Cruel and sudden, hast thou since
Purpled thy nail, in blood of innocence?
Wherein could this flea guilty be,
Except in that drop which it sucked from thee?
Yet thou triumph'st, and say'st that thou
Find'st not thyself, nor me the weaker now;
   'Tis true, then learn how false, fears be;
    Just so much honour, when thou yield'st to me,
    Will waste, as this flea's death took life from thee.

The Curse

*W*hoever guesses, thinks, or dreams he knows
Who is my mistress, wither by this curse;
      His only, and only his purse
      May some dull heart to love dispose,
And she yield then to all that are his foes;
   May he be scorned by one, whom all else scorn,
   Forswear to others, what to her he hath sworn,
   With fear of missing, shame of getting, torn:

Madness his sorrow, gout his cramp, may he
Make, by but thinking who hath made him such:
      And may he feel no touch
      Of conscience, but a fame, and be
Anguished not that 'twas sin, but that 'twas she:
   In early and long scarceness may he rot,
   For land which had been his, if he had not
   Himself incestuously an heir begot:

May he dream treason, and believe, that he
Meant to perform it, and confess, and die,
      And no record tell why:
      His sons, which none of his may be,
Inherit nothing but his infamy:
   Or may he so long parasites have fed,
   That he would fain be theirs, whom he hath bred,
   And at the last be circumcized for bread:

The venom of all stepdames, gamesters' gall,
What tyrants, and their subjects interwish,
      What plants, mines, beasts, fowl, fish,
      Can contribute, all ill which all
Prophets, or poets spake; and all which shall
   Be annexed in schedules unto this by me,
   Fall on that man; for if it be a she
   Nature before hand hath out-cursed me.

[34]

The Message

Send home my long strayed eyes to me,
Which O! too long have dwelt on thee;
Yet since there they have learned such ill,
    Such forced fashions,
    And false passions,
       That they be
       Made by thee
Fit for no good sight, keep them still.

Send home my harmless heart again,
Which no unworthy thought could stain;
But if it be taught by thine
    To make jestings
    Of protestings,
       And cross both
       Word and oath,
Keep it, for then 'tis none of mine.

Yet send me back my heart and eyes,
That I may know, and see thy lies,
And may laugh and joy, when thou
    Art in anguish
    And dost languish
       For some one
       That will none,
Or prove as false as thou art now.

A Nocturnal upon St. Lucy's Day,

'Tis the year's midnight, and it is the day's,
Lucy's, who scarce seven hours herself unmasks;
   The Sun is spent, and now his flasks
    Send forth light squibs, no constant rays;
      The world's whole sap is sunk:
The general balm th' hydroptic earth hath drunk,
Whither, as to the bed's-feet, life is shrunk,
Dead and interred; yet all these seem to laugh,
Compared with me, who am their epitaph.

Study me then, you who shall lovers be
At the next world, that is, at the next Spring:
   For I am every dead thing,
    In whom love wrought new alchemy.
      For his art did express
A quintessence even from nothingness,
From dull privations, and lean emptiness:
He ruined me, and I am re-begot
Of absence, darkness, death; things which are not.

All others, from all things, draw all that's good,
Life, soul, form, spirit, whence they being have;
   I, by love's limbec, am the grave
    Of all, that's nothing. Oft a flood
      Have we two wept, and so
Drowned the whole world, us two; oft did we grow
To be two Chaoses, when we did show
Care to aught else; and often absences
Withdrew our souls, and made us carcases.

But I am by her death (which word wrongs her)
Of the first nothing, the elixir grown;
   Were I a man, that I were one,
    I needs must know; I should prefer,
      If I were any beast,
Some ends, some means; yea plants, yea stones detest,
And love; all, all some properties invest;
If I an ordinary nothing were,
As shadow, a light, and body must be here.

But I am none; nor will my Sun renew.
You lovers, for whose sake, the lesser Sun
   At this time to the Goat is run
   To fetch new lust, and give it you,
     Enjoy your summer all;
Since she enjoys her long night's festival,
Let me prepare towards her, and let me call
This hour her Vigil, and her Eve, since this
Both the year's, and the day's deep midnight is.

Witchcraft by a Picture

I fix mine eye on thine, and there
   Pity my picture burning in thine eye,
My picture drowned in a transparent tear,
    When I look lower I espy;
      Hadst thou the wicked skill
By pictures made and marred, to kill,
How many ways mightst thou perform thy will?

But now I have drunk thy sweet salt tears,
   And though thou pour more I'll depart;
My picture vanished, vanish fears,
    That I can be endamaged by that art;
      Though thou retain of me
One picture more, yet that will be,
Being in thine own heart, from all malice free.

The Bait

Come live with me, and be my love,
And we will some new pleasures prove
Of golden sands, and crystal brooks,
With silken lines, and silver hooks.

There will the river whispering run
Warmed by thy eyes, more than the Sun.
And there th' enamoured fish will stay,
Begging themselves they may betray.

When thou wilt swim in that live bath,
Each fish, which every channel hath,
Will amorously to thee swim,
Gladder to catch thee, than thou him.

If thou, to be so seen, beest loth,
By Sun, or Moon, thou darkenest both,
And if myself have leave to see,
I need not their light, having thee.

Let others freeze with angling reeds,
And cut their legs, with shells and weeds,
Or treacherously poor fish beset,
With strangling snare, or windowy net:

Let coarse bold hands, from slimy nest
The bedded fish in banks out-wrest,
Or curious traitors, sleeve-silk flies
Bewitch poor fishes' wandering eyes.

For thee, thou need'st no such deceit,
For thou thyself art thine own bait;
That fish, that is not catched thereby,
Alas, is wiser far than I.

The Apparition

When by thy scorn, O murderess, I am dead,
And that thou think'st thee free
From all solicitation from me,
Then shall my ghost come to thy bed,
And thee, feigned vestal, in worse arms shall see;
Then thy sick taper will begin to wink,
And he, whose thou art then, being tired before,
Will, if thou stir, or pinch to wake him, think
    Thou call'st for more,
And in false sleep will from thee shrink,
And then poor aspen wretch, neglected thou
Bathed in a cold quicksilver sweat wilt lie
    A verier ghost than I;
What I will say, I will not tell thee now,
Lest that preserve thee; and since my love is spent,
I'd rather thou shouldst painfully repent,
Than by my threatenings rest still innocent.

The Broken Heart

*H*e is stark mad, who ever says,
  That he hath been in love an hour,
Yet not that love so soon decays,
  But that it can ten in less space devour;
Who will believe me, if I swear
That I have had the plague a year?
    Who would not laugh at me, if I should say,
    I saw a flask of powder burn a day?

Ah, what a trifle is a heart,
  If once into Love's hands it come!
All other griefs allow a part
  To other griefs, and ask themselves but some;
They come to us, but us Love draws,
He swallows us, and never chaws:
    By him, as by chained shot, whole ranks do die,
    He is the tyrant pike, our hearts the fry.

If 'twere not so, what did become
  Of my heart, when I first saw thee?
I brought a heart into the room,
  But from the room, I carried none with me:
If it had gone to thee, I know
Mine would have taught thine heart to show
    More pity unto me: but Love, alas,
    At one first blow did shiver it as glass.

Yet nothing can to nothing fall,
  Nor any place be empty quite,
Therefore I think my breast hath all
  Those pieces still, though they be not unite;
And now as broken glasses show
A hundred lesser faces, so
    My rags of heart can like, wish, and adore,
    But after one such love, can love no more.

[41]

A Valediction: Forbidding Mourning

As virtuous men pass mildly away,
  And whisper to their souls, to go,
Whilst some of their sad friends do say,
  The breath goes now, and some say, no:

So let us melt, and make no noise,
  No tear-floods, nor sigh-tempests move,
'Twere profanation of our joys
  To tell the laity our love.

Moving of the earth brings harms and fears,
  Men reckon what it did and meant,
But trepidation of the spheres,
  Though greater far, is innocent.

Dull sublunary lovers' love
  (Whose soul is sense) cannot admit
Absence, because it doth remove
  Those things which elemented it.

But we by a love, so much refined,
  That ourselves know not what it is,
Inter-assured of the mind,
  Care less eyes, lips, and hands to miss.

Our two souls therefore, which are one,
  Though I must go, endure not yet
A breach, but an expansion,
  Like gold to aery thinness beat.

If they be two, they are two so
  As stiff twin compasses are two,
Thy soul the fixed foot, makes no show
  To move, but doth, if th' other do.

And though it in the centre sit,
   Yet when the other far doth roam,
It leans, and hearkens after it,
   And grows erect, as that comes home.

Such wilt thou be to me, who must
   Like th' other foot, obliquely run;
Thy firmness draws my circle just,
   And makes me end, where I begun.

The Ecstasy

*W*here, like a pillow on a bed,
   A pregnant bank swelled up, to rest
The violet's reclining head,
   Sat we two, one another's best.

Our hands were firmly cemented
   With a fast balm, which thence did spring,
Our eye-beams twisted, and did thread
   Our eyes, upon one double string;

So to intergraft our hands, as yet
   Was all the means to make us one,
And pictures in our eyes to get
   Was all our propagation.

As 'twixt two equal armies, Fate
   Suspends uncertain victory,
Our souls, (which to advance their state,
   Were gone out,) hung 'twixt her, and me.

And whilst our souls negotiate there,
   We like sepulchral statues lay;
All day, the same our postures were,
   And we said nothing, all the day.

If any, so by love refined,
   That he soul's language understood,
And by good love were grown all mind,
   Within convenient distance stood,

He (though he knew not which soul spake,
   Because both meant, both spake the same)
Might thence a new concoction take,
   And part far purer than he came.

[44]

This ecstasy doth unperplex
    (We said) and tell us what we love,
We see by this, it was not sex,
    We see, we saw not what did move:

But as all several souls contain
    Mixture of things, they know not what,
Love these mixed souls doth mix again,
    And makes both one, each this and that.

A single violet transplant,
    The strength, the colour, and the size,
(All which before was poor, and scant,)
    Redoubles still, and multiplies.

When love, with one another so
    Interinanimates two souls,
That abler soul, which thence doth flow,
    Defects of loneliness controls.

We then, who are this new soul, know,
    Of what we are composed, and made,
For, th' atomies of which we grow,
    Are souls, whom no change can invade.

But O alas, so long, so far
    Our bodies why do we forbear?
They are ours, though they are not we, we are
    The intelligences, they the spheres.

We owe them thanks, because they thus,
    Did us, to us, at first convey,
Yielded their forces, sense, to us,
    Nor are dross to us, but allay.

On man heaven's influence works not so,
  But that it first imprints the air,
So soul into the soul may flow,
  Though it to body first repair.

As our blood labours to beget
  Spirits, as like souls as it can,
Because such fingers need to knit
  That subtle knot, which makes us man:

So must pure lovers' souls descend
  To affections, and to faculties,
Which sense may reach and apprehend,
  Else a great Prince in prison lies.

To our bodies turn we then, that so
  Weak men on love revealed may look;
Love's mysteries in souls do grow,
  But yet the body is his book,

And if some lover, such as we,
  Have heard this dialogue of one,
Let him still mark us, he shall see
  Small change, when we're to bodies gone.

Love's Deity

I long to talk with some old lover's ghost,
  Who died before the god of Love was born:
I cannot think that he, who then loved most,
  Sunk so low, as to love one which did scorn.
But since this god produced a destiny,
And that vice-nature, custom, lets it be;
  I must love her, that loves not me.

Sure, they which made him god, meant not so much,
  Nor he, in his young godhead practised it.
But when an even flame two hearts did touch,
  His office was indulgently to fit
Actives to passives. Correspondency
Only his subject was; it cannot be
  Love, till I love her, that loves me.

But every modern god will now extend
  His vast prerogative, as far as Jove.
To rage, to lust, to write to, to commend,
  All is the purlieu of the god of Love.
Oh were we wakened by this tyranny
To ungod this child again, it could not be
  I should love her, who loves not me.

Rebel and atheist too, why murmur I,
  As though I felt the worst that love could do?
Love might make me leave loving, or might try
  A deeper plague, to make her love me too,
Which, since she loves before, I'm loth to see;
Falsehood is worse than hate; and that must be,
  If she whom I love, should love me.

Love's Diet

*T*o what a cumbersome unwieldiness
And burdenous corpulence my love had grown,
 But that I did, to make it less,
 And keep it in proportion,
Give it a diet, made it feed upon
That which love worst endures, *discretion.*

Above one sigh a day I allowed him not,
Of which my fortune, and my faults had part;
 And if sometimes by stealth he got
 A she sigh from my mistress' heart,
And thought to feast on that, I let him see
'Twas neither very sound, nor meant to me.

If he wrung from me a tear, I brined it so
With scorn or shame, that him it nourished not;
 If he sucked hers, I let him know
 'Twas not a tear, which he had got,
His drink was counterfeit, as was his meat;
For, eyes which roll towards all, weep not, but sweat.

Whatever he would dicate, I writ that,
But burnt my letters; when she writ to me,
 And that that favour made him fat,
 I said, if any title be
Conveyed by this, ah, what doth it avail,
To be the fortieth name in an entail?

Thus I reclaimed my buzzard love, to fly
At what, and when, and how, and where I choose
 Now negligent of sport I lie,
 And now as other falconers use,
I spring a mistress, swear, write, sigh and weep:
And the game killed, or lost, go talk, and sleep.

The Will

Before I sigh my last gasp, let me breathe,
  Great love, some legacies; Here I bequeath
  Mine eyes to *Argus,* if mine eyes can see,
  If they be blind, then Love, I give them thee;
  My tongue to fame; to ambassadors mine ears;
    To women or the sea, my tears.
  Thou, Love, hast taught me heretofore
 By making me serve her who had twenty more,
That I should give to none, but such, as had too much before.

  My constancy I to the planets give;
  My truth to them, who at the Court do live;
  Mine ingenuity and openness,
  To Jesuits; to buffoons my pensiveness;
  My silence to any, who abroad hath been;
    My money to a Capuchin.
  Thou Love taughtest me, by appointing me
 To love there, where no love received can be,
Only to give to such as have an incapacity.

  My faith I give to Roman Catholics;
  All my good works unto the schismatics
  Of Amsterdam: my best civility
  And courtship, to an university;
  My modesty I give to soldiers bare;
    My patience let gamesters share.
  Thou Love taught'st me, by making me
 Love her that holds my love disparity,
Only to give to those that count my gifts indignity.

I give my reputation to those
Which were my friends; mine industry to foes;
To schoolmen I bequeath my doubtfulness;
My sickness to physicians, or excess;
To Nature, all that I in rhyme have writ;
    And to my company my wit.
Thou Love, by making me adore
Her, who begot this love in me before,
Taught'st me to make, as though I gave, when I did but
    restore.

To him for whom the passing bell next tolls,
I give my physic books; my written rolls
Of moral counsels, I to Bedlam give;
My brazen medals, unto them which live
In want of bread; to them which pass among
    All foreigners, mine English tongue.
Thou, Love, by making me love one
Who thinks her friendship a fit portion
For younger lovers, dost my gifts thus disproportion.

Therefore I'll give no more; but I'll undo
The world by dying; because love dies too.
Then all your beauties will be no more worth
Than gold in mines, where none doth draw it forth;
And all your graces no more use shall have
    Than a sun-dial in a grave.
Thou Love taught'st me, by making me
Love her, who doth neglect both me and thee,
To invent, and practise this one way, to annihilate all three.

The Funeral

Whoever comes to shroud me, do not harm
   Nor question much
That subtle wreath of hair, which crowns my arm;
The mystery, the sign you must not touch,
   For 'tis my outward soul,
Viceroy to that, which then to heaven being gone,
   Will leave this to control,
And keep these limbs, her provinces, from dissolution.

For if the sinewy thread my brain lets fall
   Through every part,
Can tie those parts, and make me one of all;
These hairs which upward grew, and strength and art
   Have from a better brain,
Can better do it; except she meant that I
   By this should know my pain,
As prisoners then are manacled, when they're condemned
    to die.

Whate'er she meant by it, bury it with me,
   For since I am
Love's martyr, it might breed idolatry,
If into others' hands these Relics came;
   As 'twas humility
To afford to it all that a Soul can do,
   So, 'tis some bravery,
That since you would save none of me, I bury some of you.

[51]

The Blossom

Little think'st thou, poor flower,
    Whom I have watched six or seven days,
And seen thy birth, and seen what every hour
Gave to thy growth, thee to this height to raise,
And now dost laugh and triumph on this bough,
        Little think'st thou
That it will freeze anon, and that I shall
Tomorrow find thee fallen, or not at all.

    Little think'st thou, poor heart,
        That labour'st yet to nestle thee,
And think'st by hovering here to get a part
In a forbidden or forbidding tree,
And hopest her stiffness by long siege to bow:
        Little thinkest thou,
That thou tomorrow, ere that Sun doth wake,
Must with this Sun, and me a journey take.

    But thou which lov'st to be
        Subtle to plague thyself, wilt say,
Alas, if you must go, what's that to me?
Here lies my business, and here I will stay:
You go to friends, whose love and means present
        Various content
To your eyes, ears, and tongue, and every part.
If then your body go, what need you a heart?

    Well, then stay here; but know,
        When thou hast stayed and done thy most;
A naked thinking heart, that makes no show,
Is to a woman, but a kind of ghost;
How shall she know my heart; or having none,
        Know thee for one?
Practice may make her know some other part,
But take my word, she doth not know a heart.

Meet me at London, then,
   Twenty days hence, and thou shalt see
Me fresher, and more fat, by being with men,
Than if I had stayed still with her and thee.
For God's sake, if you can, be you so too:
       I would give you
There, to another friend, whom we shall find
As glad to have my body, as my mind.

The Primrose, Being at Montgomery Castle, upon the Hill, on Which It Is Situate

*U*pon this primrose hill,
    Where, if Heaven would distil
A shower of rain, each several drop might go
To his own primrose, and grow Manna so;
And where their form, and their infinity
    Make a terrestrial galaxy,
    As the small stars do in the sky:
I walk to find a true love; and I see
That 'tis not a mere woman, that is she,
But must or more or less than woman be.

    Yet know I not, which flower
    I wish; a six, or four;
For should my true love less than woman be,
She were scarce anything; and then, should she
Be more than woman, she would get above
    All thought of sex, and think to move
    My heart to study her, and not to love;
Both these were monsters; since there must reside
Falsehood in woman, I could more abide,
She were by art, than nature falsified.

    Live primrose then, and thrive
    With thy true number five;
And women, whom this flower doth represent,
With this mysterious number be content;
Ten is the farthest number; if half ten
    Belong unto each woman, then
    Each woman may take half us men;
Or if this will not serve their turn, since all
Numbers are odd, or even, and they fall
First into this, five, women may take us all.

The Relic

*W*hen my grave is broken up again
    Some second guest to entertain,
    (for graves have learned that woman-head
    To be to more than one a bed)
        And he that digs it, spies
A bracelet of bright hair about the bone,
        Will he not let us alone,
And think that there a loving couple lies,
Who thought that this device might be some way
To make their souls, at the last busy day,
Meet at this grave, and make a little stay?

    If this fall in a time, or land,
    Where mis-devotion doth command,
    Then, he that digs us up, will bring
    Us, to the Bishop, and the King,
        To make us relics; then
Thou shalt be a Mary Magdalen, and I
        A something else thereby;
All women shall adore us, and some men;
And since at such time, miracles are sought,
I would have that age by this paper taught
What miracles we harmless lovers wrought.

    First, we loved well and faithfully,
    Yet knew not what we loved, nor why,
    Difference of sex no more we knew,
    Than our guardian angels do;
        Coming and going, we
Perchance might kiss, but not between those meals;
        Our hands ne'er touched the seals,
Which nature, injured by late law, sets free:
These miracles we did; but now alas,
All measure, and all language, I should pass,
Should I tell what a miracle she was.

The Damp

*W*hen I am dead, and doctors know not why,
        And my friends' curiosity
Will have me cut up to survey each part,
When they shall find your picture in my heart,
        You think a sudden damp of love
        Will through all their senses move,
And work on them as me, and so prefer
Your murder, to the name of massacre.

Poor victories! But if you dare be brave,
        And pleasure in your conquest have,
First kill the enormous Giant, your *Disdain,*
And let the enchantress *Honour,* next be slain,
        And like a Goth and Vandal rise,
        Deface records, and histories
Of your own arts and triumphs over men,
And without such advantage kill me then.

For I could muster up as well as you
        My giants, and my witches too,
Which are vast *Constancy,* and *Secretness,*
But these I neither look for, nor profess;
        Kill me as woman, let me die
        As a mere man; do you but try
Your passive valour, and you shall find then,
Naked you have odds enough of any man.

The Dissolution

She's dead; and all which die
  To their first elements resolve;
And we were mutual elements to us,
      And made of one anther.
  My body then doth hers involve,
And those things whereof I consist, hereby
In me abundant grow, and burdenous,
      And nourish not, but smother.
  My fire of passion, sighs of air,
Water of tears, and earthy sad despair,
      Which my materials be,
But near worn out by love's security,
She, to my loss, doth by her death repair,
  And I might live long wretched so
But that my fire doth with my fuel grow.
      Now as those active kings
  Whose foreign conquest treasure brings,
Receive more, and spend more, and soonest break:
This (which I am amazed that I can speak)
      This death, hath with my store
        My use increased.
And so my soul more earnestly released,
Will outstrip hers; as bullets flown before
A latter bullet may o'ertake, the powder being more.

A Jet Ring Sent

*T*hou art not so black as my heart,
  Nor half so brittle as her heart, thou art;
What would'st thou say? shall both our properties by thee
      be spoke,
  Nothing more endless, nothing sooner broke?

  Marriage rings are not of this stuff;
    Oh, why should aught less precious, or less tough
Figure our loves? Except in thy name thou have bid it say,
  I'm cheap, and naught but fashion, fling me away.

  Yet stay with me since thou art come,
    Circle this finger's top, which didst her thumb.
Be justly proud, and gladly safe, that thou dost dwell with
      me,
  She that, Oh, broke her faith, would soon break thee.

Negative Love

I never stooped so low, as they
Which on an eye, cheek, lip, can prey,
   Seldom to them, which soar no higher
   Than virtue or the mind to admire,
For sense, and understanding may
   Know, what gives fuel to their fire:
My love, though silly, is more brave,
For may I miss, whene'er I crave,
If I know yet what I would have.

If that be simply perfectest
Which can by no way be expressed
   But *Negatives,* my love is so.
   To all, which all love, I say no.
If any who decipher best,
   What we know not, ourselves, can know,
Let him teach me that nothing; this
As yet my ease, and comfort is,
Though I speed not, I cannot miss.

The Prohibition

*T*ake heed of loving me,
At least remember, I forbade it thee;
Not that I shall repair my unthrifty waste
Of breath and blood, upon thy sighs, and tears,
By being to thee then what to me thou wast;
But so great joy our life at once outwears,
Then, lest thy love, by my death, frustrate be,
If thou love me, take heed of loving me.

Take heed of hating me,
Or too much triumph in the victory.
Not that I shall be mine own officer,
And hate with hate again retaliate;
But thou wilt lose the style of conqueror,
If I, thy conquest, perish by thy hate.
Then, lest my being nothing lessen thee,
If thou hate me, take heed of hating me.

Yet, love and hate me too,
So, these extremes shall neither's office do;
Love me, that I may die the gentler way;
Hate me, because thy love is too great for me;
Or let these two, themselves, not me decay;
So shall I, live, thy stage, not triumph be;
Lest thou thy love and hate and me undo,
To let me live, O love and hate me too.

The Expiration

So, so, break off this last lamenting kiss,
   Which sucks two souls, and vapours both away;
Turn thou ghost that way, and let me turn this,
   And let ourselves benight our happiest day;
We asked none leave to love; nor will we owe
   Any, so cheap a death, as saying, Go;

Go; and if that word have not quite killed thee,
   Ease me with death, by bidding me go too.
Oh, if it have, let my word work on me,
   And a just office on a murderer do.
Except it be too late, to kill me so,
   Being double dead, going, and bidding, Go.

The Computation

For the first twenty years, since yesterday,
  I scarce believed, thou could'st be gone away,
For forty more, I fed on favours past,
  And forty on hopes, that thou would'st, they might last.
Tears drowned one hundred, and sighs blew out two,
  A thousand, I did neither think, nor do,
  Or not divide, all being one thought of you;
  Or in a thousand more, forget that too.
Yet call not this long life; but think that I
Am, by being dead, immortal; can ghosts die?

The Paradox

No Lover saith, I love, nor any other
    Can judge a perfect lover;
He thinks that else none can, nor will agree
    That any loves but he:
I cannot say I loved, for who can say
    He was killed yesterday?
Love with excess of heat, more young than old,
    Death kills with too much cold;
We die but once, and who loved last did die,
    He that saith twice, doth lie:
For though he seems to move, and stir a while,
    It doth the sense beguile.
Such life is like the light which bideth yet
    When the light's life is set,
Or like the heat, which fire in solid matter
    Leaves behind, two hours after.
Once I loved and died; and am now become
    Mine epitaph and tomb.
Here dead men speak their last, and so do I;
    Love-slain, lo, here I lie.

Farewell to Love

Whilst yet to prove,
I thought there was some deity in love
   So did I reverence, and gave
Worship; as atheists at their dying hour
Call, what they cannot name, an unknown power,
    As ignorantly did I crave:
        Thus when
Things not yet known are coveted by men,
    Our desires give them fashion, and so
As they wax lesser, fall, as they size, grow.

      But, from late fair
His highness sitting in a golden chair,
   Is not less cared for after three days
By children, than the thing which lovers so
Blindly admire, and with such worship woo;
    Being had, enjoying it decays:
        And thence,
What before pleased them all, takes but one sense
    And that so lamely, as it leaves behind
A kind of sorrowing dullness to the mind.

     Ah cannot we,
As well as cocks and lions jocund be,
   After such pleasures? Unless wise
Nature decreed (since each such Act, they say,
Diminisheth the length of life a day)
    This, as she would man would despise
        The sport;
Because that other curse of being short,
    And only for a minute made to be,
Eagers desire to raise posterity.

Since so, my mind
Shall not desire what no man else can find,
    I'll no more dote and run
To pursue things which had endamaged me.
And when I come where moving beauties be,
    As men do when the summer's sun
                Grows great,
Though I admire their greatness, shun their heat;
    Each place can afford shadows. If all fail,
'Tis but applying worm-seed to the tail.

A Lecture upon the Shadow

Stand still, and I will read to thee
A Lecture, love, in love's philosophy.
    These three hours that we have spent,
    Walking here, two shadows went
Along with us, which we ourselves produced;
But, now the Sun is just above our head,
    We do those shadows tread;
    And to brave clearness all things are reduced.
  So whilst our infant loves did grow,
  Disguises did, and shadows, flow,
  From us, and our cares; but, now 'tis not so.

That love hath not attained the highest degree,
Which is still diligent lest others see.

Except our loves at this noon stay,
We shall new shadows make the other way.
    As the first were made to blind
    Others; these which come behind
Will work upon ourselves, and blind our eyes.
If our loves faint, and westwardly decline;
    To me thou, falsely, thine,
    And I to thee mine actions shall disguise.
  The morning shadows wear away,
  But these grow longer all the day,
  But oh, love's day is short, if love decay.

Love is growing, or full constant light;
And his first minute, after noon, is night.

Sonnet: The Token

Send me some token, that my hope may live,
  Or that my easeless thoughts may sleep and rest;
Send me some honey to make sweet my hive,
  That in my passion I may hope the best.
I beg no riband wrought with thine own hands,
  To knit our loves in the fantastic strain
Of new-touched youth; nor ring to show the stands
  Of our affection, that as that's round and plain,
So should our loves meet in simplicity.
  No, nor the corals which thy wrist enfold,
Laced up together in congruity,
  To show our thoughts should rest in the same hold;
No, nor thy picture, though most gracious,
  And most desired, because best like the best;
Nor witty lines, which are most copious,
  Within the writings which thou hast addressed.

Send me nor this, nor that, to increase my store,
But swear thou think'st I love thee, and no more.

Self-Love

He that cannot choose but love,
And strives against it still,
Never shall my fancy move;
For he loves 'gainst his will;
Nor he which is all his own,
And can at pleasure choose,
When I am caught he can be gone,
And when he list refuse.
Nor he that loves none but fair,
For such by all are sought;
Nor he that can for foul ones care,
For his judgment then is naught:
Nor he that hath wit, for he
Will make me his jest or slave;
Nor a fool, for when others . . .
He can neither . . .
Nor he that still his mistress pays,
For she is thralled therefore:
Nor he that pays not, for he says.
Within, she's worth no more.
Is there then no kind of men
Whom I may freely prove?
I will vent that humour then
In mine own self-love.

Song

Stay, oh sweet, and do not rise,
The light that shines comes from thine eyes;
The day breaks not, it is my heart,
Because that you and I must part.
    Stay, or else my joys will die,
      And perish in their infancie.

Jealousy

Fond woman, which wouldst have thy husband die,
And yet complain'st of his great jealousy;
If swoln with poison, he lay in his last bed,
His body with a sere-bark covered,
Drawing his breath, as thick and short, as can
The nimblest crocheting musician,
Ready with loathsome vomiting to spew
His soul out of one hell, into a new,
Made deaf with his poor kindred's howling cries,
Begging with a few feigned tears, great legacies,
Thou wouldst not weep, but jolly, and frolic be,
As a slave, which tomorrow should be free;
Yet weep'st thou, when thou seest him hungerly
Swallow his own death, heart's-bane jealousy.
O give him many thanks, he is courteous,
That in suspecting kindly warneth us.
We must not, as we used, flout openly,
In scoffing riddles, his deformity;
Nor at his board together being sat,
With words, nor touch, scarce looks adulterate.
Nor when he swoln and pampered with great fare
Sits down, and snorts, caged in his basket chair,
Must we usurp his own bed any more,
Nor kiss and play in his house, as before.
Now I see many dangers; for that is
His realm, his castle, and his diocese.
But if, as envious men, which would revile
Their Prince, or coin his gold, themselves exile
Into another country, and do it there,
We play in another house, what should we fear?
There we will scorn his household policies,
His silly plots, and pensionary spies,
As the inhabitants of Thames' right side
Do London's Mayor; or Germans, the Pope's pride.

The Anagram

Marry, and love thy *Flavia,* for, she
Hath all things, whereby others beauteous be,
For, though her eyes be small, her mouth is great,
Though they be ivory, yet her teeth be jet,
Though they be dim, yet she is light enough,
And though her harsh hair fall, her skin is rough;
What though her cheeks be yellow, her hair is red,
Give her thine, and she hath a maidenhead.
These things are beauty's elements, where these
Meet in one, that one must, as perfect, please.
If red and white and each good quality
Be in thy wench, ne'er ask where it doth lie.
In buying things perfumed, we ask, if there
Be musk and amber in it, but not where.
Though all her parts be not in the usual place,
She hath yet an anagram of a good face.
If we might put the letters but one way,
In the lean dearth of words, what could we say?
When by the gamut some musicians make
A perfect song, others will undertake,
By the same gamut changed, to equal it.
Things simply good, can never be unfit.
She's fair as any, if all be like her,
And if none be, then she is singular.
All love is wonder; if we justly do
Account her wonderful, why not lovely too?
Love built on beauty, soon as beauty, dies;
Choose this face, changed by no deformities.
Women are all like angels; the fair be
Like those which fell to worse; but such as she,
Like to good angels, nothing can impair:
'Tis less grief to be foul, than to have been fair.
For one night's revels, silk and gold we choose,
But, in long journeys, cloth, and leather use.

Beauty is barren oft; best husbands say,
There is best land, where there is foulest way.
Of what a sovereign plaster will she be,
If thy past sins have taught thee jealousy!
Here needs no spies, nor enuchs; her commit
Safe to thy foes; yea, to a marmoset.
When Belgia's cities, the round countries drown,
That dirty foulness guards, and arms the town:
So doth her face guard her; and so, for thee,
Which, forced by business, absent oft must be,
She, whose face, like clouds, turns the day to night,
Who, mightier than the sea, makes Moors seem white,
Who, though seven years, she in the stews had laid,
A nunnery durst receive, and think a maid,
And though in childbed's labour she did lie,
Midwives would swear, 'twere but a tympany,
Whom, if she accuse herself, I credit less
Than witches, which impossible confess,
Whom dildoes, bedstaves, and her velvet glass
Would be as loth to touch as Joseph was:
One like none, and liked of none, fittest were,
For, things in fashion every man will wear.

Change

Although thy hand and faith, and good works too,
Have sealed thy love which nothing should undo,
Yea though thou fall back, that apostasy
Confirm thy love; yet much, much I fear thee.
Women are like the arts, forced unto none,
Open to all searchers, unprized, if unknown.
If I have caught a bird, and let him fly,
Another fowler using these means, as I,
May catch the same bird; and, as these things be,
Women are made for men, not him, nor me.
Foxes and goats, all beasts change when they please,
Shall women, more hot, wily, wild than these,
Be bound to one man, and did Nature then
Idly make them apter to endure than men?
They're our clogs, not their own; if a man be
Chained to a galley, yet the galley's free;
Who hath a plough-land, casts all his seed corn there,
And yet allows his ground more corn should bear;
Though Danuby into the sea must flow,
The sea receives the Rhine, Volga, and Po.
By nature, which gave it, this liberty
Thou lov'st, but Oh! canst thou love it and me?
Likeness glues love: and if that thou so do,
To make us like and love, must I change too?
More than thy hate, I hate it, rather let me
Allow her change, than change as oft as she,
And so not teach, but force my opinion
To love not any one, nor every one.
To live in one land, is captivity,
To run all countries, a wild roguery;
Waters stink soon, if in one place they bide,
And in the vast sea are more putrefied:
But when they kiss one bank, and leaving this
Never look back, but the next bank do kiss,
Then are they purest; change is the nursery
Of music, joy, life and eternity.

The Perfume

*O*nce, and but once found in thy company,
All thy supposed escapes are laid on me;
And as a thief at bar, is questioned there
By all the men, that have been robbed that year,
So am I, (by this traitorous means surprised)
By thy hydroptic father catechized
Though he had wont to search with glazed eyes,
As though he came to kill a cockatrice,
Though he hath oft sworn, that he would remove
Thy beauty's beauty, and food of our love,
Hope of his goods, if I with thee were seen,
Yet close and secret, as our souls, we have been.
Though thy immortal mother which doth lie
Still buried in her bed, yet will not die,
Takes this advantage to sleep out day-light,
And watch thy entries, and returns all night,
And, when she takes thy hand, and would seem kind,
Doth search what rings, and armlets she can find,
And kissing notes the colour of thy face,
And fearing lest thou art swoln, doth thee embrace;
To try if thou long, doth name strange meats,
And notes thy paleness, blushing, sighs, and sweats;
And politicly will to thee confess
The sins of her own youth's rank lustiness;
Yet love these sorceries did remove, and move
Thee to gull thine own mother for my love.
Thy little brethren, which like faery sprites
Oft skipped into our chamber, those sweet nights,
And kissed, and ingled on thy father's knee,
Were bribed next day, to tell what they did see:
The grim eight-foot-high iron-bound serving-man,
That oft names God in oaths, and only then,
He that to bar the first gate, doth as wide
As the great Rhodian Colossus stride,
Which, if in hell no other pains there were,

Makes me fear hell, because he must be there:
Though by thy father he were hired to this,
Could never witness any touch or kiss.
But Oh, too common ill, I brought with me
That, which betrayed me to my enemy:
A loud perfume, which at my entrance cried
Even at thy father's nose, so were we spied.
When, like a tyrant king, that in his bed
Smelt gunpowder, the pale wretch shivered.
Had it been some bad smell, he would have thought
That his own feet, or breath, that smell had wrought.
But as we in our isle imprisoned,
Where cattle only, and diverse dogs are bred,
The precious unicorns, strange monsters call,
So thought he good, strange, that had none at all.
I taught my silks, their whistling to forbear,
Even my oppressed shoes, dumb and speechless were,
Only thou bitter-sweet, whom I had laid,
Next me, me traitorously hast betrayed,
And unsuspected hast invisibly
At once fled unto him, and stayed with me.
Base excrement of earth, which dost confound
Sense, from distinguishing the sick from sound;
By thee the silly amorous sucks his death
By drawing in a leprous harlot's breath;
By thee, the greatest stain to man's estate
Falls on us, to be called effeminate;
Though you be much loved in the prince's hall,
There, things that seem, exceed substantial.
Gods, when ye fumed on altars, were pleased well,
Because you were burnt; not that they liked your smell;
You're loathsome all, being taken simply alone,
Shall we love ill things joined, and hate each one?
If you were good, your good doth soon decay;
And you are rare, that takes the good away.
All my perfumes, I give most willingly
To embalm thy father's corpse; What? will he die?

His Picture

*H*ere take my picture; though I bid farewell,
Thine, in my heart, where my soul dwells, shall dwell.
'Tis like me now, but I dead, 'twill be more
When we are shadows both, than 'twas before.
When weather-beaten I come back; my hand,
Perhaps with rude oars torn, or sun-beams tanned,
My face and breast of haircloth, and my head
With care's rash sudden storms being o'erspread,
My body a sack of bones, broken within,
And powder's blue stains scatter'd on my skin;
If rival fools tax thee to have loved a man,
So foul, and coarse, as Oh, I may seem then,
This shall say what I was: and thou shalt say,
Do his hurts reach me? doth my worth decay?
Or do they reach his judging mind, that he
Should now love less, what he did love to see?
That which in him was fair and delicate,
Was but the milk, which in love's childish state
Did nurse it: who now is grown strong enough
To feed on that, which to disused tastes seems tough.

Elegy

Oh, let me not serve so, as those men serve
Whom honour's smokes at once fatten and starve;
Poorly enriched with great men's words or looks;
Nor so write my name in thy loving books
Their princes' styles with many realms fulfil
As those idolatrous flatterers, which still
Whence they no tribute have, and where no sway.
Such services I offer as shall pay
Themselves, I hate dead names: Oh then let me
Favourite in ordinary, or no favourite be.
When my soul was in her own body, sheathed,
Nor yet by oaths betrothed, nor kisses breathed
Into my purgatory, faithless thee,
Thy heart seemed wax, and steel thy constancy:
So, careless flowers strowed on the water's face,
The curled whirlpools suck, smack, and embrace,
Yet drown them; so, the taper's beamy eye
Amorously twinkling, beckons the giddy fly,
Yet burns his wings; and such the devil is,
Scarce visiting them, who are entirely his.
When I behold a stream, which, from the spring,
Doth with doubtful melodious murmuring,
Or in a speechless slumber, calmly ride
Her wedded channel's bosom, and then chide
And bend her brows, and swell if any bough
Do but stoop down, or kiss her upmost brow:
Yet, if her often gnawing kisses win
The traitorous bank to gape, and let her in,
She rusheth violently, and doth divorce
Her from her native, and her long-kept course,
And roars, and braves it, and in gallant scorn,
In flattering eddies promising return,
She flouts the channel, who thenceforth is dry;
Then say I; that is she, and this am I.
Yet let not thy deep bitterness beget

Careless despair in me, for that will whet
My mind to scorn; and Oh, love dulled with pain
Was ne'er so wise, nor well armed as disdain.
Then with new eyes I shall survey thee, and spy
Death in thy cheeks, and darkness in thine eye.
Though hope bred faith and love: thus taught, I shall.
As nations do from Rome, from thy love fall.
My hate shall outgrow thine, and utterly
I will renounce thy dalliance: and when I
Am the recusant, in that resolute state,
What hurts it me to be excommunicate?

Elegy

Nature's lay Idiot, I taught thee to love
And in that sophistry, Oh, thou dost prove
Too subtle: Fool, thou didst not understand
The mystic language of the eye nor hand:
Nor couldst thou judge the difference of the air
Of sighs, and say, this lies, this sounds despair:
Nor by the eye's water call a malady
Desperately hot, or changing feverously.
I had not taught thee then, the alphabet
Of flowers, how they devisefully being set
And bound up, might with speechless secrecy
Deliver errands mutely, and mutually.
Remember since all thy words used to be
To every suitor; *Ay, if my friends agree;*
Since, household charms, thy husband's name to teach,
Were all the love-tricks, that thy wit could reach;
And since, an hour's discourse could scarce have made
One answer in thee, and that ill arrayed
In broken proverbs, and torn sentences.
Thou art not by so many duties his,
That from the world's common having severed thee,
Inlaid thee, neither to be seen, nor see,
As mine: who have with amorous delicacies
Refined thee into a blissful paradise.
Thy graces and good words my creatures be;
I planted knowledge and life's tree in thee,
Which Oh, shall strangers taste? Must I alas
Frame and enamel plate, and drink in Glass?
Chafe wax for others' seals? break a colt's force
And leave him then, being made a ready horse?

The Comparison

As the sweet sweat of roses in a still,
As that which from chafed musk cat's pores doth trill,
As the almighty balm of the early East,
Such are the sweat drops of my mistress' breast,
And on her brow her skin such lustre sets,
They seem no sweat drops, but pearl coronets.
Rank sweaty froth thy mistress' brow defiles,
Like spermatic issue of ripe menstruous boils,
Or like the scum, which, by need's lawless law
Enforced, Sanserra's starved men did draw
From parboiled shoes, and boots, and all the rest
Which were with any soveriegn fatness blest,
And like vile lying stones in saffroned tin,
Or warts, or weals, they hang upon her skin.
Round as the world's her head, on every side,
Like to the fatal ball which fell on Ide,
Or that whereof God had such jealousy,
As for the ravishing thereof we die.
Thy head is like a rough-hewn statue of jet,
Where marks for eyes, nose, mouth, are yet scarce set;
Like the first Chaos, or flat seeming face
Of Cynthia, when the earth's shadows her embrace.
Like Proserpine's white beauty-keeping chest,
Or Jove's best fortune's urn, is her fair breast.
Thine's like worm-eaten trunks, clothed in seal's skin,
Or grave, that's dust without, and stink within.
And like that slender stalk, at whose end stands
The woodbine quivering, are her arms and hands.
Like rough-barked elmboughs, or the russet skin
Of men late scourged for madness, or for sin,
Like Sun-parched quarters on the city gate,
Such is thy tanned skin's lamentable state.
And like a bunch of ragged carrots stand
The short swoln fingers of thy gouty hand.

Then like the chemic's masculine equal fire,
Which in the limbec's warm womb doth inspire
Into th' earth's worthless dirt a soul of gold,
Such cherishing heat her best loved part doth hold.
Thine's like the dread mouth of a fired gun,
Or like hot liquid metals newly run
Into clay moulds, or like to that Aetna
Where round about the grass is burnt away.
Are not your kisses than as filthy, and more,
As a worm sucking an envenomed sore?
Doth not thy fearful hand in feeling quake,
As one which gathering flowers, still fears a snake?
Is not your last act harsh, and violent,
As when a plough a stony ground doth rent?
So kiss good turtles, so devoutly nice
Are priests in handling reverent sacrifice,
And such in searching wounds the surgeon is
As we, when we embrace, or touch, or kiss.
Leave her, and I will leave comparing thus,
She and comparisons are odious.

The Autumnal

No Spring, nor summer beauty hath such grace,
   As I have seen in one autumnal face.
Young beauties force our love, and that's a rape,
   This doth but counsel, yet you cannot scape.
If 'twere a shame to love, here 'twere no shame,
   Affection here takes reverence's name.
Were her first years the Golden Age; that's true,
   But now she's gold oft tried, and ever new.
That was her torrid and inflaming time,
   This is her tolerable tropic clime.
Fair eyes, who asks more heat than comes from hence,
   He in a fever wishes pestilence.
Call not these wrinkles, graves; If graves they were,
   They were Love's graves; for else he is no where.
Yet lies not Love dead here, but here doth sit
   Vowed to this trench, like an Anachorite.
And here, till hers, which must be his death, come,
   He doth not dig a grave, but build a tomb.
Here dwells he, though he sojourn everywhere,
   In progress, yet his standing house is here.
Here, where still evening is; not noon, nor night;
   Where no voluptuousness, yet all delight.
In all her words, unto all hearers fit,
   You may at revels, you at council, sit.
This is love's timber, youth his underwood;
   There he, as wine in June, enrages blood,
Which then comes seasonabliest, when our taste
   And appetite to other things is past.
Xerxes' strange Lydian love, the Platane tree,
   Was loved for age, none being so large as she,
Or else because, being young, nature did bless
   Her youth with age's glory, barrenness.
If we love things long sought, age is a thing
   Which we are fifty years in compassing;

If transitory things, which soon decay,
  Age must be loveliest at the latest day.
But name not winter-faces, whose skin's slack;
  Lank, as an unthrift's purse; but a soul's sack;
Whose eyes seek light within, for all here's shade;
  Whose mouths are holes, rather worn out, than made;
Whose every tooth to a several place is gone,
  To vex their souls at Resurrection;
Name not these living death's-heads unto me,
  For these, not ancient, but antique be.
I hate extremes; yet I had rather stay
  With tombs, than cradles, to wear out a day.
Since such love's natural lation is, may still
My love descend, and journey down the hill,
Not panting after growing beauties, so,
  I shall ebb out with them, who homeward go.

The Dream

*I*mage of her whom I love, more than she,
   Whose fair impression in my faithful heart,
Makes me her medal, and makes her love me,
   As kings do coins, to which their stamps impart
The value: go, and take my heart from hence.
   Which now is grown too great and good for me:
Honours oppress weak spirits, and our sense
   Strong objects dull; the more, the less we see.
When you are gone, and reason gone with you,
   Then fantasy is queen and soul, and all;
She can present joys meaner than you do;
   Convenient, and more proportional.
So, if I dream I have you, I have you,
   For, all our joys are but fantastical.
And so I scape the pain, for pain is true;
   And sleep which locks up sense, doth lock out all.
After a such fruition I shall wake,
   And, but the waking, nothing shall repent;
And shall to love more thankful sonnets make,
   Than if more honour, tears, and pains were spent.
But dearest heart, and dearer image, stay;
   Alas, true joys at best are dream enough;
Though you stay here you pass too fast away:
   For even at first life's taper is a snuff.
Filled with her love, may I be rather grown
Mad with much heart, than idiot with none.

The Bracelet

*Upon the loss of his Mistress' Chain for which he
made satisfaction*

Nor that in colour it was like thy hair,
For armlets of that thou mayst let me wear;
Nor that thy hand it oft embraced and kissed,
For so it had that good, which oft I missed:
Nor for that silly old morality,
That as these links were knit, our love should be:
Mourn I that I thy sevenfold chain have lost;
Nor for the luck sake; but the bitter cost.
Oh, shall twelve righteous angels, which as yet
No leaven of vile solder did admit;
Nor yet by any way have strayed or gone
From the first state of their creation;
Angels, which heaven commanded to provide
All things to me, and be my faithful guide;
To gain new friends, to appease great enemies;
To comfort my soul, when I lie or rise;
Shall these twelve innocents, by thy severe
Sentence (dread judge) my sins' great burden bear?
Shall they be damned, and in the furnace thrown,
And punished for offences not their own?
They save not me, they do not ease my pains,
When in that hell they're burnt and tied in chains.
Were they but crowns of France, I cared not,
For, most of these, their natural country's rot
I think possesseth, they come here to us,
So pale, so lame, so lean, so ruinous;
And howsoe'er French kings most Christian be,
Their crowns are circumcised most Jewishly.
Or were they Spanish stamps, still travelling,
That are become as Catholic as their king,
Those unlicked bear-whelps, unfiled pistolets
That (more than cannon shot) avails or lets;

[85]

Which negligently felt unrounded, look
Like many-angled figures, in the book
Of some great Conjurer that would enforce
Nature, as these do justice, from her course;
Which, as the soul quickens head, feet and heart,
As streams, like veins, run through the earth's every part,
Visit all countries, and have slily made
Gorgeous *France,* ruined, ragged and decayed;
Scotland, which knew no State, proud in one day:
And mangled seventeen-headed *Belgia.*
Or were it such gold as that wherewithal
Almighty chemics from each mineral
Having by subtle fire a soul out-pulled,
Are dirtily and desperately gulled:
I would not spit to quench the fire they're in,
For, they are guilty of much heinous sin.
But, shall my harmless angels perish? Shall
I lose my guard, my ease, my food, my all?
Much hope which they should nourish will be dead,
Much of my able youth, and lustihead
Will vanish; if thou love let them alone,
For thou wilt love me less when they are gone;
And be content that some loud speaking crier
Well-pleased with one lean thread-bare groat, for hire
May like a devil roar through every street;
And gall the finder's conscience, if they meet.
Or let me creep to some dread conjurer,
That with fantastic schemes fills full much paper;
Which hath divided heaven in tenements,
And with whores, thieves, and murderers stuffed his rents.
So full, that though he pass them all in sin,
He leaves himself no room to enter in.
But if, when all his art and time is spent,
He say 'twill ne'er be found; yet be content;
Receive from him that doom ungrudgingly,
Because he is the mouth of destiny.

Thou say'st (alas) the gold doth still remain,
Though it be changed, and put into a chain;
So in the first fall'n angels, resteth still
Wisdom and knowledge; but, 'tis turned to ill:
As these should do good works; and should provide
Necessities; but now must nurse thy pride.
And they are still bad angels; mine are none;
For, form gives being, and their form is gone:
Pity these angels; yet their dignities
Pass virtues, powers, and principalities.
      But, thou art resolute; thy will be done!
Yet with such anguish, as her only son
The mother in the hungry grave doth lay,
Unto the fire these martyrs I betray.
Good souls, (for you give life to everything)
Good angels, (for good messages you bring)
Destined you might have been to such an one,
As would have loved and worshipped you alone:
One that would suffer hunger, nakedness,
Yea, death, ere he would make your number less.
But, I am guilty of your sad decay;
May your few fellows longer with me stay.
      But Oh thou wretched finder whom I hate
So, that I almost pity thy estate:
Gold being the heaviest metal amongst all,
May my most heavy curse upon thee fall:
Here fettered, manacled, and hanged in chains,
First mayst thou be; then chained to hellish pains;
Or be with foreign gold bribed to betray
Thy country, and fail both of that and thy pay,
May the next thing thou stoop'st to reach, contain
Poison, whose nimble fume rot thy moist brain;
Or libels, or some interdicted thing,
Which negligently kept, thy ruin bring.
Lust-bred diseases rot thee; and dwell with thee
Itchy desire, and no ability.

May all the evils that gold ever wrought;
All mischiefs that all devils ever thought;
Want after plenty; poor and gouty age;
The plagues of travellers; love; marriage
Afflict thee, and at thy life's last moment,
May thy swoln sins themselves to thee present.
    But, I forgive; repent thee honest man:
Gold is restorative, restore it then:
But if from it thou be'st loth to depart,
Because 'tis cordial, would 'twere at thy heart.

His Parting from Her

Since she must go, and I must mourn, come Night,
Environ me with darkness, whilst I write:
Shadow that hell unto me, which alone
I am to suffer when my love is gone.
Alas the darkest magic cannot do it,
Thou and great hell to boot are shadows to it.
Should Cynthia quit thee, Venus, and each star,
It would not form one thought dark as mine are.
I could lend thee obscureness now, and say,
Out of my self, there should be no more day,
Such is already my felt want of sight,
Did not the fires within me force a light.
O Love, that fire and darkness should be mixed,
Or to thy Triumphs so strange torments fixed!
Is not because thou thyself art blind, that we
Thy martyrs must no more each other see?
Or takest thou pride to break us on the wheel,
And view old chaos in the pains we feel
Or have we left undone some mutual rite,
Through holy fear, that merits thy despite?
No, no. The fault was mine, impute it to me,
Or rather to conspiring destiny,
Which (since I loved for form before) decreed,
That I should suffer when I loved indeed:
And therefore now, sooner than I can say,
I saw the golden fruit, 'tis rapt away.
Or as I had watched one drop in a vast stream,
And I left wealthy only in a dream.
Yet Love, thou art blinder than thyself in this,
To vex my dove-like friend for my amiss:
And, where my own sad truth may expiate
Thy wrath, to make her fortune run my fate:
So blinded Justice doth, when favourites fall,
Strike them, their house, their friends, their followers all.

Was 't not enough, that thou didst dart thy fires
Into our bloods, inflaming our desires,
And madest us sigh and glow, and pant, and burn,
And then thyself into our flame didst turn?
Was 't not enough, that thou didst hazard us
To paths in love so dark, so dangerous:
And those so ambushed round with household spies,
And over all, thy husband's towering eyes
That flamed with oily sweat of jealousy:
Yet went we not still on with constancy?
Have we not kept our guards, like spy on spy?
Had correspondence whilst the foe stood by?
Stolen (more to sweeten them) our many blisses
Of meetings, conference, embracements, kisses?
Shadowed with negligence our most respects?
Varied our language through all dialects,
Of becks, winks, looks, and often under-boards
Spoke dialogues with our feet far from our words?
Have we proved all these secrets of our art,
Yea, thy pale inwards, and thy panting heart?
And, after all this passed purgatory,
Must sad divorce make us the vulgar story?
First let our eyes be riveted quite through
Our turning brains, and both our lips grow to:
Let our arms clasp like ivy, and our fear
Freeze us together, that we may stick here,
Till fortune, that would rive us, with the deed,
Strain her eyes open, and it make them bleed.
For Love it cannot be, whom hitherto
I have accused, should such a mischief do.
O fortune, thou art not worth my least exclaim
And plague enough thou hast in my own shame.
Do thy great worst, my friend and I have arms,
Though not against thy strokes, against thy harms
Rend us in sunder, thou canst not divide
Our bodies so, but that our souls are tied,
And we can love by letters still and gifts,

And thoughts and dreams; Love never wanteth shifts.
I will not look upon the quickening Sun,
But straight her beauty to my sense shall run;
The air shall note her soft, the fire most pure;
Water suggest her clear, and the earth sure.
Time shall not lose our passages; the Spring
How fresh our love was in the beginning;
The Summer how it ripened in the ear;
And Autumn, what our golden harvests were.
The Winter I'll not think on to spite thee,
But count it a lost season, so shall she.
And dearest friend, since we must part, drown night
With hope of day, burthens well borne are light.
Though cold and darkness longer hang somewhere,
Yet Phoebus equally lights all the sphere.
And what he cannot in like portions pay,
The world enjoys in mass, and so we may.
Be then ever yourself, and let no woe
Win on your health, your youth, your beauty: so
Declare yourself base fortune's enemy,
No less by your contempt than constancy;
That I may grow enamoured on your mind,
When my own thoughts I there reflected find.
For this to the comfort of my dear I vow,
My deeds shall still be what my words are now;
The Poles shall move to teach me ere I start;
And when I change my Love, I'll change my heart;
Nay, if I wax but cold in my desire,
Think, heaven hath motion lost, and the world, fire:
Much more I could, but many words have made
That, oft, suspected which men would persuade;
Take therefore all in this: I love so true,
As I will never look for less in you.

On His Mistress

By our first strange and fatal interview,
By all desires which thereof did ensue,
By our long starving hopes, by that remorse
Which my words' masculine persuasive force
Begot in thee, and by the memory
Of hurts, which spies and rivals threatened me,
I calmly beg: but by thy father's wrath,
By all pains, which want and divorcement hath,
I conjure thee, and all the oaths which I
And thou have sworn to seal joint constancy,
Here I unswear, and overswear them thus,
Thou shalt not love by ways so dangerous.
Temper, O fair love, love's impetuous rage,
Be my true mistress still, not my feigned page;
I'll go, and, by thy kind leave, leave behind
Thee, only worthy to nurse in my mind
Thirst to come back; O if thou die before,
My soul from other lands to thee shall soar.
Thy (else almighty) beauty cannot move
Rage from the seas, nor thy love teach them love,
Nor tame wild Boreas' harshness; thou hast read
How roughly he in pieces shivered
Fair Orithea, whom he swore he loved.
Fall ill or good, 'tis madness he have proved.
Dangers unurged; feed on this flattery,
That absent Lovers one in the other be.
Dissemble nothing, not a boy, nor change
Thy body's habit, nor mind's; be not strange
To thyself only; all will spy in thy face
A blushing womanly discovering grace;
Richly clothed Apes, are called Apes, and as soon
Eclipsed as bright we call the Moon the Moon.
Men of France, changeable chameleons,
Spitals of diseases, shops of fashions,

Love's fuellers, and the rightest company
Of players, which upon the world's stage be,
Will quickly know thee, and no less, alas!
The indifferent Italian, as we pass
His warm land, well content to think thee page,
Will hunt thee with such lust, and hideous rage,
As Lot's fair guests were vexed. But none of these
Nor spongy hydroptic Dutch shall thee displease,
If thou stay here. O stay here, for, for thee
England is only a worthy gallery,
To walk in expectation, till from thence
Our greatest King call thee to his presence.
When I am gone, dream me some happiness,
Nor let thy looks our long-hid love confess,
Nor praise, nor dispraise me, nor bless nor curse
Openly love's force, nor in bed fright thy nurse
With midnight's startings, crying out, oh, oh
Nurse, O my love is slain, I saw him go
O'er the white Alps alone; I saw him, I,
Assailed, fight, taken, stabbed, bleed, fall, and die.
Augur me better chance, except dread Jove
Think it enough for me to have had thy love.

Love's Progress

Whoever loves, if he do not propose
The right true end of love, he's one that goes
To sea for nothing but to make him sick:
Love is a bear-whelp born, if we o'er-lick
Our love, and force it new strange shapes to take,
We err, and of a lump a monster make.
Were not a calf a monster that were grown
Faced like a man, though better than his own?
Perfection is in unity: prefer
One woman first, and then one thing in her.
I, when I value gold, may think upon
The ductileness, the application,
The wholesomeness, the ingenuity,
From rust, from soil, from fire ever free:
But if I love it, 'tis because 'tis made
By our new nature use the soul of trade.

   All these in women we might think upon
(If women had them) and yet love but one.
Can men more injure women than to say
They love them for that, by which they're not they?
Makes virtue woman? must I cool my blood
Till I both be, and find one wise and good?
May barren angels love so. But if we
Make love to woman; virtue is not she:
As beauty's not nor wealth: he that strays thus
From her to hers, is more adulterous
Than if he took her maid. Search every sphere
And firmament, our *Cupid* is not there:
He's an infernal god and underground
With *Pluto* dwells, where gold and fire abound:
Men to such gods, their sacrificing coals
Did not in altars lay, but pits and holes.
Although we see Celestial bodies move
Above the earth, the earth we till and love:

So we her airs contemplate, words and heart,
And virtues; but we love the centric part.

   Nor is the soul more worthy, or more fit
For love, than this, as infinite as it.
But in attaining this desired place
How much they err, that set out at the face?
The hair a forest is of ambushes,
Of springs, snares, fetters and manacles:
The brow becalms us when 'tis smooth and plain,
And when 'tis wrinkled, shipwrecks us again.
Smooth, 'tis a paradise, where we would have
Immortal stay, and wrinkled 'tis our grave.
The nose (like to the first meridian) runs
Not 'twixt an East and West, but 'twixt two suns;
It leaves a cheek, a rosy hemisphere
On either side, and then directs us where
Upon the islands fortunate we fall,
(Not faint *Canaries,* but ambrosial)
Her swelling lips; to which when we are come,
We anchor there, and think ourselves at home,
For they seem all: there sirens' songs, and there
Wise Delphic Oracles do fill the ear;
There in a creek where chosen pearls do swell,
The remora, her cleaving tongue doth dwell.
These, and the glorious promontory, her chin
O'erpast; and the strait *Hellespont* between
The *Sestos* and *Abydos* of her breasts,
(Not of two lovers, but two loves the nests)
Succeeds a boundless sea, but yet thine eye
Some island moles may scattered there descry;
And sailing towards her *India,* in that way
Shall at her fair Atlantic navel stay;
Though thence the current be thy pilot made,
Yet ere thou be where thou wouldst be embay'd,
Thou shalt upon another forest set,
Where many shipwreck, and no further get.

When thou art there, consider what this chase
Misspent by thy beginning at the face.
    Rather set out below; practise my art,
Some symmetry the foot hath with that part
Which thou dost seek, and is thy map for that
Lovely enough to stop, but not stay at:
Least subject to disguise and change it is;
Men say the Devil never can change his.
It is the emblem that hath figured
Firmness; 'tis the first part that comes to bed.
Civility we see refined: the kiss
Which at the face began, transplanted is,
Since to the hand, since to the imperial knee,
Now at the Papal foot delights to be:
If kings think that the nearer way, and do
Rise from the foot, lovers may do so too;
For as free spheres move faster far than can
Birds, whom the air resists, so may that man
Which goes this empty and ethereal way,
Than if at beauty's elements he stay.
Rich Nature hath in women wisely made
Two purses, and their mouths aversely laid:
They then, which to the lower tribute owe,
That way which that exchequer looks, must go:
He which doth not, his error is as great,
As who by Clyster gave the stomach meat.

To His Mistress Going to Bed

Come, Madam, come, all rest my powers defy,
Until I labour, I in labour lie.
The foe oft-times having the foe in sight,
Is tired with standing though he never fight.
Off with that girdle, like heaven's zone glistering,
But a far fairer world encompassing.
Unpin that spangled breastplate which you wear,
That th' eyes of busy fools may be stopt there.
Unlace yourself, for that harmonious chime.
Tells me from you, that now it is bed time.
Off with that happy busk, which I envy,
That still can be, and still can stand so nigh.
Your gown going off, such beauteous state reveals,
As when from flowry meads the hill's shadow steals.
Off with that wiry coronet and show
The hairy diadem which on you doth grow:
Now off with those shoes, and then safely tread
In this love's hallowed temple, this soft bed.
In such white robes, heaven's angels used to be
Received by men; thou angel bring'st with thee
A heaven like Mahomet's Paradise; and though
Ill spirits walk in white, we easily know,
By this these angels from an evil sprite,
Those set our hairs, but these our flesh upright.

  Licence my roving hands, and let them go,
Before, behind, between, above, below.
O my America! my new-found-land,
My kingdom, safeliest when with one man manned,
My mine of precious stones, My empery,
How blest am I in this discovering thee!
To enter in these bonds, is to be free;
Then where my hand is set, my seal shall be.

  Full nakedness! All joys are due to thee,
As souls unbodied, bodies unclothed must be,
To taste whole joys. Gems which you women use

Are like Atlanta's balls, cast in men's views,
That when a fool's eye lighteth on a gem,
His earthly soul may covet theirs, not them.
Like pictures, or like books' gay coverings made
For lay-men, are all women thus arrayed;
Themselves are mystic books, which only we
(Whom their imputed grace will dignify)
Must see revealed. Then since that I may know,
As liberally, as to a midwife, show
Thyself: cast all, yea, this white linen hence,
There is no penance due to innocence.

    To teach thee, I am naked first; why then
What needst thou have more covering than a man.

Love's War

*T*ill I have peace with thee, war other men,
And when I have peace, can I leave thee then?
All other wars are scrupulous; only thou
O fair free city, may'st thyself allow
To any one. In Flanders, who can tell
Whether the master press; or men rebel?
Only we know, that which all idiots say,
They bear most blows which come to part the fray.
France in her lunatic giddiness did hate
Ever our men, yea and our God of late;
Yet she relies upon our angels well,
Which ne'er return; no more than they which fell.
Sick Ireland is with a strange war possessed
Like to an ague; now raging, now at rest;
Which time will cure: yet it must do her good
If she were purged, and her head-vein let blood.
And Midas' joys our Spanish journeys give,
We touch all gold, but find no food to live.
And I should be in the hot parching clime,
To dust and ashes turned before my time.
To mew me in a ship, is to enthral
Me in a prison, that were like to fall;
Or in a cloister; save that there men dwell
In a calm heaven, here in a swaggering hell.
Long voyages are long consumptions,
And ships are carts for executions.
Yea they are deaths; is't not all one to fly
Into an other world, as 'tis to die?
Here let me war; in these arms let me lie;
Here let me parley, batter, bleed, and die.
Thine arms imprison me, and mine arms thee,
Thy heart thy ransom is, take mine for me.
Other men war that they their rest may gain;
But we will rest that we may fight again.

Those wars the ignorant, these th' experienced love,
There we are always under, here above.
There engines far off breed a just true fear,
Near thrusts, pikes, stabs, yea bullets hurt not here.
There lies are wrongs; here safe uprightly lie;
There men kill men, we'll make one by and by.
Thou nothing; I not half so much shall do
In these wars, as they may which from us two
Shall spring. Thousands we see which travel not
To wars, but stay swords, arms, and shot
To make at home; and shall not I do then
More glorious service, staying to make men?